# The Great British Woodstock

# The Great British Woodstock

## The Incredible Story of the Weeley Festival 1971

### Ray Clark

The
History
Press

Once again my wife, Shelley, has helped, encouraged and attempted to ease my literary frustrations in the strange and incomprehensible art of punctuation as I've been writing my second and last book – until the next one. Thank you x

*Frontispiece*: **Festival fans.** (Dick Farrow)

First published 2017
Reprinted 2020, 2024

The History Press
97 St George's Place,
Cheltenham, Gloucestershire, GL50 3QB
www.thehistorypress.co.uk

British Library Cataloguing in Publication Data.
A catalogue record for this book is available from the British Library.

ISBN 978 0 7509 6989 5

Typesetting and origination by The History Press
Printed by TJ Books Limited, Padstow, Cornwal

# CONTENTS

# ABOUT THE AUTHOR

Ray Clark has enjoyed a successful radio career for more than thirty years. He has been heard on a number of radio stations and is one of the few people to have presented the breakfast show on pirate, commercial, BBC and American radio. He has won numerous radio awards throughout the years and has produced a number of radio documentaries on various topics, including the Weeley Festival.

Ray currently presents radio programmes for BBC Essex and Radio Caroline.

His first book, *Radio Caroline: The True Story of the Boat That Rocked*, is published by The History Press.

**Beautiful weather at Weeley.** (Dick Farrow)

# ACKNOWLEDGEMENTS

I've found the subject of the Weeley Festival fascinating since buying my ticket for the event in 1971. I was just 17 years old, but my interest in the festival hasn't diminished in the nearly fifty years since. Before embarking on a career in radio, my work took me through Weeley on a weekly timetable – quite literally, as I drove the bus through the village. Gazing across the fields of Hall Farm continues to be an addictive sight and I still imagine the 150,000 people who temporarily moved into the area.

Some years later, as I was looking for an idea for a radio documentary, my friend and radio colleague Tim Gillett mentioned the approaching 35th anniversary of the festival, which prompted me to start my research into the Weeley phenomenon. Many of those who witnessed and were involved in the festival have been very welcoming and helpful beyond words, and I'd like to express my grateful thanks to them. They include 'Dr Dick', Dick Farrow, whose passion when talking about Weeley and generous loan of scarce photographs have been hugely appreciated. Thanks, also, to former Clacton Round Table members Graham Syrett and Nigel Davers. Weeley baker Hoss Selfe has also been very supportive of the idea.

Without help from the following, the odds of the story of Weeley ever being written would be unlikely.

My very grateful thanks go to Aynsley Davidson and James Dwan from the *Clacton and Frinton Gazette* for permission to use photographs and references to the festival from the former *East Essex Gazette*, which covered the event comprehensively at the time, not least due to excellent reports written by Mike Sams.

The Essex Police Museum has supplied a treasure chest of information and documents relating to Weeley. Curator Becky Wash has been so helpful, and the museum, which is open to the public, has a fascinating collection of all things police.

Thanks, also, to the many others who spoke to me about their Weeley experiences, especially Garry Bodenham and Kevin Herridge, who kindly allowed permission to use their wonderful photographs.

Wherever possible I have spoken about events with those involved at the time, but in some cases (the Hells Angels court cases, for example) I have used information that was common to numerous reports from various newspaper cuttings.

Many thanks to Lauren at The History Press for her patience and understanding

Finally, although I've never met them, we should all thank the late Vic Speck and Peter Gibbs for their inspirational idea of an event to replace the annual Clacton Donkey Derby.

# FOREWORD

*The Great British Woodstock* is the story of an event organised by a group of young men with admirable intentions, but with ideas that took them completely out of their depth. They were naive in the extreme, but then this true story took place in 1971, and naivety wasn't seen as an obstacle to any endeavour in those days. They just had a great idea – an idea that ran away with them while they were clinging on, desperately trying to control it …

It happened during the early days of the decade, when everything seemed possible and where nothing could get in the way of a good idea, especially if it was being done in the name of charity. The resolve of the organisers was tested to the extreme by bureaucracy: the world of officialdom was challenged, the patience of some village residents was pushed to the limit, and most of the bad guys were beaten – there just wasn't any 'official' way to stop the event from happening. And all this was set to the music of the day in a tiny Essex settlement.

'Top pop festival planned': It was a small, sub-headline on the front page of the *East Essex Gazette* on 15 January 1971, but it was the first public announcement of Clacton Round Table's summer fundraising event for that year. The Weeley Festival of Progressive Music, and the stories surrounding it, were to become legendary for those who were there or living nearby and nationally for music fans 'of a certain age' – or maybe those that remember reading something about the place in the national newspapers at the time.

Weeley was a tiny Essex village at the start of the seventies, and it's not much bigger now. It had a population of 951 in 1971. It was, and still is, the gateway to 'the Essex sunshine coast'; the main road from everywhere diverges here. To the north of the village the road takes you to the traditional English seaside town of Walton-on-the-Naze and the more genteel Frinton-on-Sea, and to the south to Clacton-on-Sea, home, at that time, to numerous seaside hotels and the huge Butlin's holiday camp. Much has changed in the years since 1971. Weeley is now bypassed and expanding, but it's still possible to find the exact site of the festival, and to find villagers that speak positively about the most amazing event in the most unlikely of places.

'The Great British Woodstock' is a grand title, which other festivals may also lay claim to; there had been a much larger gathering of music fans just a year earlier on the Isle of Wight, for example. But the story of Weeley is different in so many ways. Organised by well-meaning amateurs, it was an event that just ran away from the local businessmen and tradespeople who formed the Clacton Round Table, which just wanted to make money for good causes and at the same time put on an event for young people. They certainly didn't start off with the expectation of playing host to around 150,000 pop fans!

# 1

# THE WAY IT WAS

At the start of the 1960s, the British music industry was practically non-existent. However, by the end of the decade the country was leading the world, with the Beatles and the Mersey Beat as the vanguard for a British music invasion. Many bands from provincial cities like Manchester, Newcastle, Birmingham and London followed Liverpool's lead. They were promoted domestically by pirate radio and later Radio 1, and on hugely popular television music shows such as *Ready Steady Go* and *Top of the Pops*, resulting in huge success.

Britain was celebrating a newfound confidence. It was now a country in which teenagers had found their voice and were intent on throwing off the shackles, and the desperate years experienced by their parents just a decade or so earlier, following the Second World War, seemed a distant memory. Throughout the Swinging Sixties, pop music had become big business, and for many youngsters it was their main interest. Being with your mates and listening to pop music was all that seemed to matter.

The British music explosion had been fed by the stars of the day appearing in cinemas in major provincial towns, with artists such as Cliff Richard and Adam Faith attracting full houses at the local Odeon. By 1963, it was The Beatles who were leading the way. Bands like The Rolling Stones, Manfred Mann and The Who followed, but as early as 1966 the Beatles had given up performing in buildings that just didn't allow fans to stand up and dance to the music that excited them so.

In minor market towns and villages, small and sweaty clubs and smaller halls at the rear of pubs played host to groups. In major towns, ballrooms hosted big name bands, but for up-and-coming acts, many of them by now playing 'psychedelic' or 'underground' music, there were few opportunities to be heard. And with the advent of supergroups such as Cream and Led Zeppelin the local Odeon was no longer suitable, while American fans could see their favourite bands in the relative comfort of football stadiums, British fans had no such luxury.

By 1967, at the height of 'flower power', the great outdoors beckoned. One of the first events took place in August that year at Woburn Abbey, where a love-in was held – heralded as 'a three-day, non-stop festival of the flower children'. Bands performing at this event included The Kinks, The Small Faces, the Bee Gees and Eric Burdon. The fans loved it, but it was more for the benefit of the music industry. Money had to be made, and more room meant more people, each paying £1 for a ticket. And such outdoor festivals offered further opportunities to generate revenue: kaftans and flowery clothing were on sale, and even a hot dog cost an unbelievable 1s 9d.

Free music festivals first appeared in London's Hyde Park in 1968, and continued through until 1971. The London parks oversaw the arrangements, but were still not particularly keen on having loud music and strange pop fans invading their normally tranquil surroundings. Over this three-year period, a who's who of rock musicians could be seen performing in the parks, with no charge to the public: Pink Floyd, Donovan, Blind Faith, Crosby, Stills and Nash, and, famously, The Rolling Stones in July 1969, only days after the death of the band's founding member, Brian Jones.

In 1969, the largest festival of the time was held on a dairy farm in New York State, USA. It took place over four days in mid August, and an estimated 400,000 music fans enjoyed performances from some of the biggest names in rock music, including Jimi Hendrix, The Who, Janis Joplin, Joe Cocker and the Grease Band, Joan Baez and Credence Clearwater Revival. The Woodstock Music and Art Fair became a landmark event, not only because its sheer scale and huge attendance, but also because it marked the culmination of counterculture trends that had shocked previous generations, including drug-taking, sexual freedom, hippie culture and anti-establishment attitudes. Woodstock had become a free festival by chance: the sheer numbers of fans attending over-whelmed any hope of organising ticket distribution and the fences surrounding the site were incomplete when the music fans started to arrive. Thunderstorms and heavy rain turned the site into a quagmire, and traffic queues brought the entire area to a standstill.

In Britain, a number of similar, if smaller, events were taking place. The Reading Festival still occurs annually; it had started as the National Jazz Festival in 1965 in Richmond, Surrey and moved to various locations before settling in the Berkshire town. Other jazz festivals had been held in the UK throughout the sixties, but none were on the scale of Woodstock, although the second festival on the Isle of Wight, which took place in August 1969, came close. Held just days after Woodstock, Bob Dylan topped the bill, which explains why he was missing from the Woodstock line-up.

However, it was the 1970 Isle of Wight Festival that hit the newspaper headlines – partly for the line-up, which included Jimi Hendrix, The Who and The Doors, and partly because attendance was estimated at over half a million. But it was the behaviour of some of the crowd that garnered the most attention. The organisers had been forced to use what they saw as an unsuitable venue because it was the only site where the authorities were prepared to allow the festival to take place; permission had been refused at their preferred sites. As a result, while the majority of those attending had paid for tickets, many thousands were able to view proceedings from vantage points outside the concert site. With organisers losing money, those outside the arena were verbally attacked from the stage, and this in turn inflamed part of the audience. A number of artist's performances were subjected to heckling and can-throwing. Although the mood eventually calmed down, there was an unpleasant atmosphere surrounding much of the festival. Many local residents were incensed at what they saw as crowds of 'unwashed hippies and thugs' taking over their quiet and neat island paradise, and with the huge numbers trying to leave for the mainland at the same time, roads throughout the island were blocked and there were chaotic scenes at the ferry terminals.

The difficulties experienced at the Isle of Wight Festival would lead to a government Act being forced through Parliament limiting any future gathering on the island to a maximum of 5,000 people. Consequently, there would be no Isle of Wight Festival in 1971 or for many years to come. A festival was successfully revived in 2002, but there is no connection between the present event and those held in the 1960s and '70s.

At many outdoor events, gangs of motorcyclists would often arrive and take on the responsibility for security, a position that they considered theirs without question. Many were members of Hell's Angels chapters, modelling themselves on the

American bikers and hellraisers they had seen on screen and in news reports; others were groups of motorcyclists who were better described as 'greasers'. Whether they were real Hell's Angels or not, these groups of leather-clad, long-haired young men on motorcycles were very intimidating when they roared on to festival sites, caring little for anyone foolish enough to get in their way. Once in a position of self-proclaimed authority, they demanded payment, either in cash or drink. It's reasonable to assume that on many occasions festival organisers were happy to do whatever it took to keep them onside. Reports of protection demands from Angels against traders at festivals were also frequently heard. The Phun City Festival, held near Worthing on the south coast of England in the summer of 1970, suffered from their attentions in particular. The festival was underfinanced, poorly organised and attracted bad press and bad feelings. Hell's Angels clashed with concessionaires and generally created a threatening atmosphere for the music fans attending. The Bath Festivals, held in 1969 and 1970, also witnessed Hells Angels in attendance – taking care of stage security, riding their ostentatious machines (often with chrome features and extended handlebars) through the crowd, being obnoxious and generally operating under a law of their own.

The mood of music festivals was changing; a threatening, aggressive undercurrent was beginning to challenge the 'love and peace' ideal of most of those attending. With organisers vying to present the biggest names in music, the cost of security was often an afterthought, and this attitude allowed the Hell's Angels, the self-styled upholders of the law, to predominate. It was a cause for concern for festival-goers, organisers and traders.

The police were always placed in a difficult position. The festivals were usually held on private property, and their job was to keep the peace, but their presence on-site was often seen to be provocative at a time when many festival-goers considered them a threat to their chosen way of life and uninhibited behaviour. And the Angels just viewed them as opponents.

# 2

# IN THE BEGINNING

Founded in 1927, Round Table is about having fun with a great bunch of mates and supporting local communities. Round Table clubs raise over £2 million a year for local charities and good causes through various events including bonfire nights, beer festivals and Santa sleigh collections. www.roundtable.co.uk

Throughout the 1960s, Clacton-on-Sea Round Table regularly held fundraising projects during the year. Its biggest event was the annual fete, held every August, which attracted locals and visiting holidaymakers, and was always a good money spinner. Numerous local charities and good causes benefitted from the donations made from the proceeds by the Round Table.

The 1970 event included a variety of attractions, notably a donkey derby, but those paying their 2s admission fee could also join in with the chance to win a goldfish and have fun on the bottle-smashing stall. It was a great success, and made several hundred pounds for Round Table funds.

The members of Clacton Round Table, all in their twenties and thirties, had become very good at running the summer fete and donkey derby. However, it was decided that the following year they would try something different:

I'd been a member of Clacton Round Table for a while. Prior to 1971, we'd been running small, local fetes and a summer fair, and for the previous year or two we'd been running a donkey derby, but I think we'd got fed up of donkeys, so we were looking for something different to do.
**Graham Syrett, Clacton Round Table**

We used to buy a giant teddy bear for a tenner, and we'd sell raffle tickets around all the holiday camps in town and we'd make about £150. Somebody got up and said, 'I'm fed up with all the time we spend on this, we'd be better off all putting in a fiver each.' Then someone suggested a boxing night, but that would have clashed with the holiday season and there'd be nowhere available to hold it.
**Nigel Davers, Clacton Round Table**

Clacton Round Table, like countless similar groups around the world, met regularly. Their meetings took place at the Carlton Hotel in the town, and would usually include a meal, followed by the business of the day, often followed by a presentation from a guest speaker. The Round Table was made up of mainly professional and self-employed men. The group was run by an organising committee with roles such as chairman, secretary and fundraising chairman. Vic Speck, a successful Clacton-based businessman, was chairman of the fundraising committee in the autumn of 1970 and was always keen to find a fresh challenge for his colleagues to get involved with:

Vic was a businessman, in his late 30s. His family had been in farming originally and he loved the land. He'd been to public school in Surrey and had been working in finance, and with his entrepreneurial skills had found a niche in the market. As the government was closing mental institutions around the country, Vic set up homes that looked after the former patients' needs. He did it properly; he followed the rule book to the letter.

**Dr Dick Farrow, Clacton GP and Clacton Round Table**

During the autumn months of 1970, an idea started to emerge to move away from the safe and assured profitability of the summer fete and to organise an event for youngsters in the area that could potentially raise far more money – not just for local charities, but to allow the Round Table to donate to national groups that would benefit youngsters in need.

Vic Speck's proposal was to hold a pop festival for the youngsters in the Clacton area. In truth, pop festival was a very grand title for what was on the table. The initial idea was for an event to be held in a field behind the Blacksmiths Arms, a pub in the village of Little Clacton, featuring local bands. It would take place during the August Bank Holiday weekend, for twelve hours through the night – giving it more credibility with youngsters. Not only would ticket sales raise funds for the club, but, in keeping with the ideals of the Round Table organisation, would involve teenagers and younger adults, a group that were seldom served by the usual events.

The son of the Weeley baker was the drummer in a local professional band called Mustard. They were successfully performing around the country and abroad:

'I was over the moon about it when I heard there was to be a pop festival here; I couldn't believe that it was true. We'd played at a fundraising event for Clacton Round Table a year or eighteen months previously, and that was when we first heard about the festival. It was going to be for local bands, such as ourselves, playing to an audience of two or three thousand maximum.

**Hoss Selfe, Weeley resident, baker and musician**

Although Vic Speck was the event's mainstay, other members of the group were also keen for the festival to go ahead. Local pharmacist and committee member Peter Gibbs was very much behind the idea and, together with Speck, took charge of selling the project to fellow Round Table members.

**Clacton Round Table's summer event for 1970.**

When it came to voting for a pop festival, most of the Round Tablers were in favour and excited about trying something new and different. At the time they were relatively young men and most relished the chance to be in the limelight. A pop event sounded fun, and the members looked forward to the different challenges that it would bring.

Originally we were going to arrange a small festival for about 2,000 people with country and folk singers. The idea was then progressed to include pop singers, and the size of the audience enlarged to about 10,000 and that was what we voted for.
**Nigel Davers, Clacton Round Table**

I'd moved from Yorkshire to join a general practice in Clacton and I'd already been a member of Round Table, so I automatically became a member of Clacton Round Table. After about the fourth meeting, Vic Speck, our fundraising chairman,

came up to me and said, 'I'm thinking of organising a pop concert in the summer, in a field somewhere. If we did, would you be able to provide a little first aid?' 'Of course,' I said. 'Yes, delighted.'
**Dr Dick Farrow, Clacton GP and Clacton Round Table**

As the logistics of organising the festival started to evolve, it was feared that the site initially selected might be too small and, because of its close proximity to houses in Little Clacton, not suitable for an event continuing through the night and featuring loud music. Local farmer and landowner Roger Weeley was then approached. He was known by many of the locals in the neighbouring village of Weeley as the squire. He offered the use of his 32-acre site on Hall Farm to the Round Table free of charge. The new venue was about 3 miles further west of the original pub site, and although close to the village the plan was to position the arena itself in a field furthest away from houses, beyond the village church and backing on to a large area of woodland.

As 1971 arrived, the Round Table decided to go public with their festival idea. The local newspaper made the announcement, with a small item on the front page:

**Top Pop Festival Planned**

A secluded 30-acre site at Weeley could provide the stage for being the biggest pop happening in north-east Essex, since the rumour that Beatle Paul McCartney visited St. Osyth with his one-time girlfriend, Jane Asher.

Yes, a mini Isle of Wight type festival.

Ten hours of continuous music by at least one nationally famous group and several local groups at £1 a head.

The festival will be held from 6pm on Saturday, August 28 until 4am the following morning.
*East Essex Gazette*, 15 January 1971

**A big field, and organisers Vic Speck and Peter Gibbs.**

Mike Sams, a junior reporter on the local newspaper, was one of the first to learn of the exciting ideas, when Clacton Round Table approached him with the sketchy details of their plans:

> There were two main organisers whom I went to see and interviewed, Vic Speck and Peter Gibbs, and they told me what they were going to do. Their idea was to put on a pop festival on a farmer's land just outside Weeley; they were trying to arrange it and could the paper help in any way?

Subsequently we printed stories and I interviewed them on many, many occasions as the pop festival idea developed and was pushed along.

As they told me of their plans, it was apparent that they had no idea. They had the passion, but they didn't know what they were doing.

They didn't know the popular bands of the time, they just thought it would be a wonderful idea and they had this marvellous vision of what a great money-spinner it would be. Normally they would hold an annual donkey derby and raise money that

**A humorous take on the festival preparations.** (*East Essex Gazette*)

" I've ploughed up every meadow in Weeley. If they still hold that pop festival they'll be knee deep in mud."

WEELEY VILLAGE HALL

POP FESTIVAL CONCEIVED 1970 DIED 1971 R.I.P WEELEY

way, but these two high-flyers, they thought, no, this year we're going to hold a pop festival. We will do it ... and they put their heart and soul into it, and their volunteers and the other members did the same.

**Mike Sams, newspaper reporter**

The reaction within the village to the news was one of shock and disbelief. A special meeting of the parish council was quickly organised, with villagers, district council and police attending. Memories of the news footage of the previous year's Isle of Wight Festival were obviously uppermost in the minds of many of the village elders, who repeatedly referred to the 'chaos and destruction' that would be coming to their quiet village. The meeting resolved to ask the Round Table to think again about the location. 'We simply do not want it,' they said. Disquiet continued throughout Weeley, while with residents and councillors from neighbouring villages were relieved that they were to avoid the problem of a pop festival within their parish.

Then, the Round Table suddenly announced that the festival was to be called off. The prohibitive cost of fulfilling the licence agreement for music and entertainment was the reason given. A mock funeral was held outside the village hall, with members of the Round Table, dressed as mourners, carrying a coffin and a replica headstone. It was the Round Table's way of letting the locals know that the idea was dead, killed by officialdom ... or was it? Could it have been a clever promotional ploy?

Just two days later, hopes that the festival would take place were revived once again. It seemed that the conditions the county council insisted on were for events held inside a construction, not on open farmland. A meeting was held between the Round Table's Vic Speck, landowner Roger Weeley and a representative of Essex County Council. An elated Vic Speck suggested the festival might be back on:

'If we find we can comply with these conditions there is every possibility that Clacton Round Table may reconsider their decision.'

The final decision was to be made in the first week of March 1971, when a meeting of the county's Special Purposes Committee heard arguments for and against the festival taking place at Hall Farm. Several opponents from the village had written to the council voicing their concerns, and a petition opposing the application was also considered:

> We can well do without this great upsurge to our rural way of life, especially as it is being got up by a lot of greedy people who are out to show how clever they are by conning the youth and upsetting a lot of old people ... to dump about the most disturbing and rowdy thing of modern times on our doorstep is, to my mind, showing a lack of thought, consideration and good sense.

One of the most vociferous opponents to the festival was Major General F.J.C. Piggot, who wasn't at all happy at the prospect of his village being overrun by people attending the festival:

> My objections include the objectionable and amplified noise; the invasion of the village by perhaps 10,000 pop fans for several days without visible means of support until the social security offices open after the Bank Holiday; the sanitary problem; and the danger to property from pilferers, or worse, which our constable will be unable to prevent.

The local assistant chief constable also attended the meeting, representing the police, whose position was not to formally oppose the granting of a licence, but rather to put forward a number of points of concern.

After a five-hour session, it was agreed (by a majority of seven votes to five) that a special music event licence be granted to landowner Roger Weeley. But there were a number of conditions, including a ruling that Clacton Round Table had to take direct control of security, and that the attendance, at the Round Table's suggestion, would be restricted to 10,000 festival-goers.

Vic Speck was jubilant and updated reporters of the plans:

> The festival site could take 25,000 pop fans and parking for 15,000 cars would be available, but only 10,000 young people, mainly from north Essex, are expected to attend. About 250 volunteers will run the festival, and a number of local pop groups and one well-known group will be performing.

One final attempt was made by a county councillor to prevent the festival going ahead by asking for a review of the decision to grant the licence, but his efforts were in vain. Concern was still being voiced at local council meetings, too, with one councillor claiming that the character of the event was changing: 'Something rather contrary to what was earlier outlined by the Tablers now seems to be in the back of their minds ... they're now even applying for a drinks licence, which earlier they had stated they would not.'

Despite these difficulties, now armed with an official 'thumbs-up' the organisers were forging ahead with preparations for the biggest Round Table event that they'd ever undertaken.

*Opposite:* **There will be NO festival: Members of Clacton Round Table mourn their festival dream.** (Dick Farrow)

# 3

# GETTIN' IT TOGETHER

Having now received official approval from the county council, the Weeley Pop Festival organising committee was able to make positive plans for the event, which was now just six months away. Members of the Round Table took on a variety of jobs that they thought necessary to run what had now become the Weeley Festival of Music:

Vic had taken the lead, as it was his idea and it was all in his head. He was the mainstay together with Peter Gibbs, the local pharmacist, and they were the two who took the lead. As GP, I was responsible for medical matters. Roy Link was a plumber, and he took charge of plumbing and water supply. Jim Thurston, an electrician, and Norman Thompson took communications, as he worked for Post Office telephones. Graham Stanford was assistant manager of the local Halifax building society branch, so he looked after concessions. The three solicitors in the club took charge of car parking.

**Dr Dick Farrow, Clacton GP and Clacton Round Table**

I started as head of security, purely because I was involved in martial arts. I had a martial arts club and they thought I'd be the ideal person for it, but as things progressed other guys became involved. All of us took part in the preparation and we never

realised what a mammoth task it was, and it was to become, but how enjoyable it would be.
**Nigel Davers, Clacton Round Table**

There had been rumours that at least one well-known pop group would be booked to appear on the stage in the field behind the church. Contact had been made with the management of Mungo Jerry, and the band was booked even before the official go-ahead had been granted.

Mungo Jerry had enjoyed huge success in the music charts the previous summer with their song 'In the Summertime'. It had become the biggest hit of the year. The sentiment of the song, played by a fun-loving, carefree group of young people, summed up the dream of the organisers. Around the same time, Dick Farrow recalls, the Round Table sensibly realised that it needed expert advice and assistance when it came to dealing with musicians and their agents – a business completely alien to the tradesmen and professionals who made up the committee. They needed someone who understood the essentials of running such an operation, which, they were just starting to realise, might become bigger than they had originally envisaged:

As the Round Table started to get the ball rolling, the festival got a bit out of hand for them, so they got hold of a promoter from, I believe, Brighton, who started taking over. And then it really started to snowball. He was bringing in big-name bands who I really couldn't believe were going to play in our tiny village.

**Hoss Selfe, Weeley resident, baker and musician**

Completely unacquainted with the way the music industry worked, the Round Table had to find someone who had access to the very people that were needed if this event was to have any sort of credibility with the youngsters it was hoping to attract to Weeley. Colin King was approached by Vic Speck. King, a flamboyant self-styled pop entrepreneur, headed a business that he called the Colin King Organisation. Based in Brighton, he had experience of music promotion and had been involved in organising several previous festivals and outdoor stage events, including both the Bath and Isle of Wight Festivals.

Well, I received a phone call from a gentleman who said he was from the Clacton Round Table and he wanted to put on an event in the summer of 1971. It was during February that he called me, and he'd heard that I had done these sorts of things.

He told me that he'd booked Mungo Jerry and that he wanted to put on a pop event; that was the way he described it, and he'd been told that I could help him. So I said, 'Well, I'll come and talk to you.' So I went down to Essex and I met him – Vic Speck – and another guy, Peter Gibbs I think it was. They said they had a 120-acre site and they wanted to put on a pop festival.

I told them that I'd help, but I didn't do small. If they wanted a small event they didn't want me. My experience was with large events, I'd been involved with the Bath Festival and the Isle of Wight Festival, so if you want a big one, then I'm the man.

They then started talking about attendance and who they should have to appear there. They said, 'We've got 120 acres, do you think we could get 10,000 people there?' I said, 'Yes, probably, 20,000, 30,000 ... as many as you want really ... it depends on your budget.' So we went away and talked about budgets. I worked out a budget for them, called them up and said, 'Well, these are the bands I can get you and this is what it'll cost you, how about it?' And they said, 'Yep, go ahead.'

**Colin King, festival show director**

Colin King got involved, he knew all the contacts and he looked the part – flamboyant. He wore all the gear with the 'Zappa' moustache and the

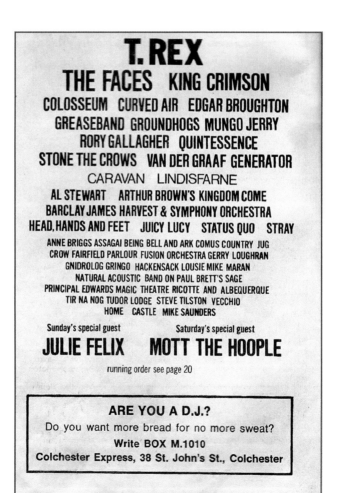

**The line-up is made public.**

high-heeled boots. Once he came on board the whole thing seemed to pick up momentum. Everything happened very quickly once he came along – in fact, too quick for some of us to grasp. There was an element of fear that it was running away with us, because we were finding out more from the local paper about what was going on than what we actually knew. It did leave a bit of an odd taste. Decisions had to be made, but we were a bit perturbed because we didn't know. It was down to communication. Nowadays we have email and mobile phones, instant decisions can be made.

We also we had the Round Table national and area groups asking, 'Do you know what you're doing, guys; can you handle it?' Yeah, we all thought we could, but if we had involved other Tables it would have been much better.'
**Graham Syrett, Clacton Round Table**

When I told the Clacton Round Table members how many we expected to attend they were shocked, and some of them were quite angry that they hadn't been kept up to date with what was happening. They were, of course, compromised and had no choice but to settle down and turn the field into a viable environment, including digging trenches for toilets, putting up marquees and building a security fence around the arena.
**Colin King, festival show director**

Once Colin King was signed up and on board, all thoughts of relying purely on local bands were dismissed. Although they were still welcome to take part, the few local bands that had arranged to play were soon overlooked as the big-name stars began lining up for the festival.

They got involved with a music promoter, and from then on one band would follow another. These bands were calling and saying 'We would like to be there …

and we would like to be there.' They were partially underground, partially progressive, I would think, but they just kept coming, one after another.
**Mike Sams, newspaper reporter**

As publicity continued to build, there was interest and offers of assistance and support from many quarters, some of them surprising. The Bishop of Colchester, hoping for a coming together of all denominations, announced plans to set up a centre for spiritual guidance on the festival site. Based in St Andrew's church, which was central to the whole festival area, it would be adjacent to both planned entrance routes for festival-goers:

'… knowing all the valuable work done at the Isle of Wight festival by the churches working in the 'Jesus tent' where people who wanted to discuss spiritual things, or simply get their fare back to London, received tremendous help.

I realise the Weeley festival will not be identical with the Isle of Wight event. I don't suppose there will be all the drop-outs and drug addicts, but I think there may be something the church can do.'
*East Essex Gazette*, 23 April 1971

### Top Pop Groups For Festival

Although names like Mungo Jerry, Marmalade, Dave Edmunds and Rockpile, Fairweather, The Equals and Status Quo may not convey much to the older generation, but they could be comparable to the combined bands of Henry Hall, Joe Loss, Jack Payne and Jack Hylton.

In short, Clacton Round Table has scooped the cream of Britain's groups for their 12-hour pop festival, the Weeley Festival of Music on August 28th.

And that's not bad for an organisation which only went into the pop business less than four months ago.
*East Essex Gazette*, 30 April 1971

Names of many more bands were announced over the following days, and it soon became obvious that someone, either the Round Table members or Colin King, was trying to impress and attract maximum publicity for the event. However, it should be noted that of those that were announced at this time, only two of them actually appeared in the line-up at the festival some months later ...

Despite Essex County Council voting to allow the event to go ahead, the licence wasn't issued until days before the event actually got underway, and the authorities were still unsure about the repercussions of having such an event in their area. A verbal agreement with Clacton Council had been made to place an advertising banner for the festival in Station Road but was then revoked, with council members saying they wanted to take another look at the whole question of support for the event. The local newspaper was very critical of the council members in their editorial:

> Pop festivals may not be everyone's idea of fun but Clacton Round Table have county approval for their venture, which, after all, is for local charity and they intend to hold it whether Clacton approves or not.
> The council's plea for a second look at the decision can only have one interpretation and that is sure to harden, and possibly widen, the generation gap of which so many complain.
> *East Essex Gazette*

But still the concerns from certain sections of officialdom continued. Fears that more than 100 police officers would have to be drafted in at a cost of £2,120 were voiced by the Essex and Southend Police Authority, and with all police leave and holidays having to be cancelled over the Bank Holiday weekend, these predictions weren't exactly unfounded.

MELODY MAKER "The Greatest Rock Event of the Year"

WEELEY FESTIVAL OF PROGRESSIVE MUSIC BANK HOLIDAY SAT/SUN AUG 28-29 TICKETS in advance £1·50 at Gate £2·00

The beautiful wooded 200-acre site at Weeley Heath opens 6 p.m Friday, 27th August. Camping and free cooking facilities. Car parking, festival village, refreshments and drinks.

T. REX . FACES . King Crimson . Curved Air . Mott the Hoople . Colosseum . Ground . Hogs . Mungo Jerry . Quintessence . Juicy Lucy . Rory Gallagher . Grease Band . Barclay James Harvest and Orchestra, Edgar Broughton

Al Stewart . Arthur Brown's Kingdom Come . Assagai . Dave Edmund's Rockpile . Tir na nog . Third Ear Band . Van der Graaf Generator . Principal Edwards Magic Theatre . ON . Lindisfarne . Kiss . Hackensack . Jerry Lockran . Demon Fuzz . Formerly Fat Harry . Gnidrolog . Argent . Bell and Arc . Stray . Steve Tilsdon . Ricotti and Alberque . Natural Acoustic Band . Louise . Gringo . Head, Hands and Feet . Caravan . Fairfield Parlour . Fusion Orchestra.

To: R.T. TICKET AGENCY
16 ALBANY GARDENS EAST, CLACTON, ESSEX
Please send me .......... tickets I enclose cheque/P O for £.............. and stamped addressed envelope

However, there were supporters on the local council: 'The Round Table does a lot of work for charity and this is a charitable exercise,' said a member. But one opponent expressed concern over what he saw as the festival growing in size: 'Who is kidding who? I have already seen reports in two national papers that could well boost the figures over the agreed 10,000. The plans and ideas of the promoters appear on the surface to have altered considerably since they understood a licence would be granted.'

Preparations continued towards the festival as the summer approached, although the fields, still weeks away from being harvested, had crops growing where the arena, camping sites, car parking areas and the administration 'village' were to be sited. The eventual line-up of bands was starting to take shape, and, unlike previous major festivals where stars had flown in (mainly from America), Weeley was to concentrate on home-grown talent:

The year before, at the Bath Festival, the bands were from around the world, it was an international festival, mostly made up of American bands, I thought it was about time that we put on a British band festival and the fact that it was for charity went down very well with the bands. It was like a precursor to Live Aid, except that the money was to stay in this country; the plan was to donate to Save the Children, Shelter and Release.

I approached Rod Stewart and Marc Bolan, Coliseum, Stone the Crows and several more, a whole raft of bands really. I wanted Pink Floyd, but they weren't in the country. They were the only band I couldn't get hold of. I didn't want Led Zeppelin as they were too expensive.

The management of these bands knew all about pop festivals, and the artists' management asked what sort of audience numbers we were going to get. I said, 'I expect around 50,000, but the people who are putting it on don't really understand what that number of people would expect.'
**Colin King, festival show director**

Although a limit of 10,000 had been agreed with the county council earlier in the year, at the suggestion of the Round Table, a letter was sent on 17 May 1971 attempting to withdraw this limit on numbers. The request was refused, but from then on it became increasingly apparent that the organisers were endeavouring to attract as large a crowd as possible.

Word was soon getting out that a very special music event was to be held in Essex. Those living in the north of the county had been made aware of the plans, with regular stories reporting the latest issues with the festival appearing in the local newspapers. However, by the end of spring, stories were starting to appear in the national music press, together with half-page advertisements for the Weeley Festival, giving details of a very impressive list of the artists expected to appear.

The original agreement had limited advertising to the local area, but now regular advertisements for the festival started to appear in magazines such as *Melody Maker*. Vic Speck was questioned about them by police at meetings prior to the festival. He said that they had been inserted by the bands themselves, although it was noted by the police that the format of the adverts in the national press were the same as those published in the local press.

Tickets were already on sale at the official box office. Pre-paid tickets were available at £1.50 and the proposed charge 'on the gate' was £2. Festival-goers were invited to send their cheque or postal order to the RT Ticket Agency; the address given was that of Round Table member and festival champion Peter Gibbs.

The tickets, printed on white card, were very simple in appearance. WEELEY FESTIVAL 71 was boldly printed above AUGUST BANK HOLIDAY WEEKEND,

ADMIT ONE, PRICE £2.00. In an attempt to stop tickets being copied and duplicated, the only visible security was a stamp from Mr Gibbs' Chemist in Great Clacton:

> 'There was considerable discussion over a long period of time about the security and printing of the tickets. They were as secure as they could be at the time; there were no watermarks available as there are today.'
> **Dr Dick Farrow, Clacton GP and Clacton Round Table**

From the start, the event was billed as 'the people's festival', taking place in a beautifully wooded site of 200 acres, 5 miles from the sea, with a camping site available, complete with cooking facilities. With the promise, 'ALL PROCEEDS TO BE GIVEN TO CHARITY. DONATIONS TO RELEASE, SHELTER AND SAVE THE CHILDREN FUND'

As Clacton Round Table pushed forward with their preparations, the county police force were taking steps to find out more about music festivals and those that attended them. A detective sergeant from Essex was sent to the Reading Blues and Pop Festival, held over the last weekend of June. His brief was to walk around and observe just what went on, and a full report of occurrences and observations from the festival was prepared in order to give the Essex force an idea of what to expect. Concern was expressed that trouble might come from Essex University students. At the time, students from the campus, just 5 miles away, had a reputation for being a rebellious group, who often protested and caused disturbances at public events:

> I would respectfully suggest careful consideration be given to employing some officers from outside forces on Drugs Squads who, I must admit, impressed me very much at the Reading Festival.

There is no doubt that at Weeley, some Essex University militants will attend and, from this point of view, some trouble may be experienced, but in any case, I would have thought, at most, 150 uniform officers could deal with any situation that may arise.
**Internal police report from officer attending Reading Festival, June 1971**

The largest gathering of people in one place in the county, prior to Weeley, was the annual Essex Show, an agricultural event held near the county town of Chelmsford. This, and the increased number of day visitors who swelled the usual population for a few weeks in summer at the county's seaside resorts, was policed by a small number of officers. Apart from dealing with a few drunks and the occasional seaside fight after the pubs closed, the major part of their duty was directing traffic. But with increasing intelligence, it was obvious that a large police presence would be required for the festival, although, as agreed with the Round Table, they would not be responsible for security on the site and would only be available to ensure the keeping of the peace should the need arise. It was agreed that specialist drugs

**A Weeley ticket, complete with box office stamp.**

officers would be on duty within the festival arena and campsite, and uniformed officers would deal with any traffic problems.

Despite agreement from the county council much earlier in the year, as the date of the festival grew closer the public entertainment licence had still not been issued; in fact it was just five days before the event started that the licence, and the strict conditions it outlined, were issued to the organisers. A number of the conditions imposed by the licence would be of considerable importance once the festival got underway:

- All vegetation within the area shall be cut back to ground level other than hedge and trees. All cuttings shall be destroyed or completely removed from the area.
- The site shall be enclosed using primarily a system of stout timber boards supported by steel scaffolding.
- The site enclosure shall be provided with a minimum of three routes of escape.
- No vehicles shall be permitted to enter the site other than for emergency purposes.
- Conditions regarding car parking, sanitation, the number of toilets and general welfare of those attending the event shall be given local attention.
- Site security shall be maintained by the organisers at all times.

The police were most concerned about security. At a meeting held at Clacton Police Station on 31 July, an outline of the proposed security arrangements was given. Peter Gibbs told officers that there were 300 volunteers for duty on the site, and additional paid helpers would add to that number, but no details of names or addresses of the helpers were available. There was also concern about parking and access to the site. Neighbouring farmer Bill Leiper told police that he had not given permission for camping on his fields, as shown in the official site plans, and, just four weeks from the festival date, he was still reluctant to allow access to the site across his land. By this time, at least 10,000 tickets had already been sold.

At the beginning of August, work on constructing the festival site started in earnest. A huge wooden fence was built around the entire arena, as well as the main stage. A backstage area was set aside for the caravans and facilities of those appearing, as well as the staff responsible for the stage presentations. Another area was designated 'the village', catering for administration, medical and religious needs, and

**Organisers' message from official programme.**

### Message from the organisers—

THIS festival is not a "Bread Trip," every penny it makes will go to aid Bangla Desh, Shelter Release and other important community charities. That means any damage done on the site, which has been given free by two local farmers, will have to be paid for out of the charity take.

We feel that the best way to say thank you to the farmers for letting us have their land is to leave it the way we found it.

### —And who they are

Promoters of the Pop Festival are Round Table vice-chairman Vic Speck and Peter Gibbs, a past chairman.

VIC SPECK, who is thirty-seven, has been a member of the Round Table for five years. Originally from Kent, he has lived in Clacton for over 20 years and has numerous business interests in the area.

PETER GIBBS, aged thirty-three, is a pharmacist and has also lived in Clacton for the past 20 years. He has been a member of the Round Table for ten years, and was its chairman in 1969.

And why has the Clacton Round Table persevered with the role it plays in business and criticism?

"Firstly as a me...

concessions offering food, drink and other goods for the festival crowds.

Local residents watched with fascination as preparations for the event took over parts of Hall Farm.

My house backed on to the pop field, and about a month before the festival they started setting up the stage. As time went on more and more people arrived; they came from everywhere, all over Europe, everywhere, and there were even some from Australia and New Zealand too, it was fantastic.

I really liked the time before it began. Why isn't the world like it now? Everybody was friends; they were promoting peace in those days. 'Love and Peace man.' It was just a lovely atmosphere.
**Ena Wade, Weeley resident**

It had become apparent within music circles and amongst regular festival-goers that Weeley had become the 'must attend' music event of the year. It had also been known for some time that there was to be no Isle of Wight Festival, but as August began news came that another festival, planned for Canterbury and to be held over the same weekend as Weeley, was to be cancelled. It later became known that the decision to cancel had been prompted by protests from none other than Weeley organiser Vic Speck. He had been concerned that the event in Kent, organised by actor Stanley Baker, would jeopardise the success of Weeley. Many of the acts booked for the Essex festival were also signed up to appear at the Canterbury event:

'There was no chance of our festival being called off – the arrangements had gone too far – but certainly it would have severely hindered our own efforts for charity.'
*East Essex Gazette*, 6 August 1971

Just days before the festival was due to take place, Vic Speck and his family suffered a tragic loss; his daughter Emma drowned in a pond at the family home in Little Clacton. But, as the major force behind the event, he saw it as his duty to continue with preparations; the event was too big to stop now.

The public opinion of Speck's pop festival idea, with a dream of raising thousands of pounds for charity and entertaining thousands of youngsters in the process, was seen as either a huge example of naivety or a great adventure that would live on in the memory of those involved.

As the festival date drew closer, local journalist Mike Sams was writing regular updates, with every day bringing new twists and turns to what was fast becoming the biggest story he'd ever covered.

Now, you had the Canterbury Festival and the Isle of Wight Festival, which were the two big ones, but they'd both been cancelled and there was nowhere for the young people to go. There were many who regularly followed the festivals. Somehow it went on the telegraph that there was going to be a festival in Essex, at somewhere called Weeley. No one knew where Weeley was, but then people started arriving, weeks before they were expected by the organisers. Consequently people started camping out on local land weeks before the final preparations were finished. I can remember the members of the Round Table working on the site, they were putting up this security fence which was completely unsuitable … well, it was so bad it wouldn't have held out a fly really. They had no idea.
**Mike Sams, newspaper reporter**

The land belonged to my father and partly to the neighbouring farm, but most of the festival was on father's land. I remember a crew coming in and working on the stage. There was a lot of scaffolding to be erected and plenty of trucks on the site and noise. This was done over a few weeks beforehand. The harvest had been done in that particular area, but it was still covered in loose straw when some of the people started to arrive. That did prove to be a bit of a hazard a bit later.

**David Weeley, Weeley resident, son of Roger Weeley, landowner**

The task of preparing the festival site was a daunting one, and as many of the Round Table members were used to working behind a desk, they were soon confronted by the huge challenge that lay before them. With all profits going to charity, huge favours had to be called in. Local companies donated many items, such as timber and marquees, but they all needed erecting, and every available pair of hands (including some of the early arrivals) was enlisted on the festival ground.

**The official police site map.** (Essex Police Museum)

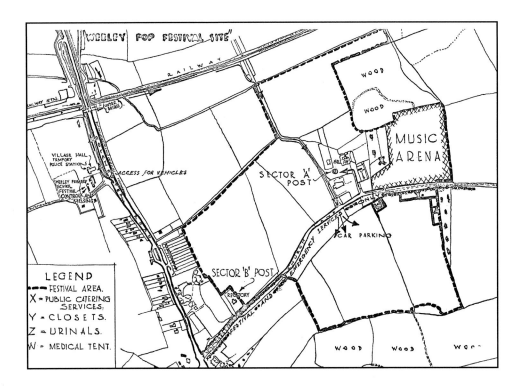

The challenge facing the construction team was immense: an area of 10 acres had to be entirely surrounded by a 6ft-high wooden fence, using more than 10,000 scaffold boards and 300 tons of scaffolding. Thirty-seven marquees had to be erected in 'the village', and a mile of water pipe was installed across the fields that formed the showground. Five generators for floodlights, tent and standby lighting for the stage were obtained and, of course, the subsequent wiring had to be connected. The stage itself was to be powered by a new 100kw electricity substation that was installed especially for the event. Eighteen standpipes were to provide water.

Sanitary arrangements were also the responsibility of the men from the Round Table, and here the creative ingenuity of the members was called upon. Anyone who attended the Weeley Festival will remember the toilets, and not with fond memories:

They were called the chicks' bogs and the boys' bogs. We cadged a trench digger from somebody, and Round Table member Roy Lint oversaw the digging of the trenches. We went to a factory in Clacton and asked if they could provide us with any sheeting to provide privacy. This guy said, 'Well, I've got some bright pink plastic rolls that I don't want.' It was a metre wide, so he gave us half a dozen rolls. We put up wooden poles and then stretched this sheeting right the way along. Then we found the tallest person on the site and asked if he could look over the top? He said, 'I suppose I could if I stood on tiptoes.' So we put some extra poles in and put another layer on top. Eventually the screens were about 9ft high, and these screens lasted the whole weekend.

**Nigel Davers, Clacton Round Table**

The ladies toilets were all positioned together and not too much of a problem. The men's toilets were a

different kettle of fish. There was a very long trench dug, probably 5ft deep, and across the trench, which must have been 50ft long, there was some scaffolding ... Number 2s were a problem, so you had to lean on the scaffolding and perch yourself, which I think was quite risky.
**Graham Syrett, Clacton Round Table**

The actual siting of the toilets, and the total number to be provided, was discussed at great length as the organisers wanted to provide only one communal trench for both sexes without any form of cover. This was not agreed to, and it was insisted that the toilets be constructed as approved.

Friday 20 August saw work progressing on the male toilet trench using an excavator. This trench was finally made 200ft long and screened from sight by plastic sheeting nailed to timber poles driven into the ground. Around the periphery of the trench, scaffolding was constructed to form a barrier to prevent persons from falling into the trench and this scaffolding in turn was used to create 200 toilets.

The female toilets were a little more refined, in that a total of 130 Elsan type buckets were arranged in two separate enclosures.
**Official site report from Essex County Council**

Despite the Round Table getting the official go-ahead earlier in the year, with just a week before the event opposition to the festival was still to be heard. Some locals continued to voice their fears, and having seeing some of the preparations they were becoming more and more justified in their concerns.

Confirmed anti-festival protestor Major General F.J. Piggot was leading a three-man subcommittee of the parish council, who produced and delivered a leaflet giving villagers advice on how to cope with the invasion of thousands of music fans.

Remove to a safe place any movable items from your garden, such as laundry, garden ornaments, bicycles and toys. Residents are advised to take in extra supplies of milk before the festival starts and to avoid leaving bottles on the doorstep.
*East Essex Gazette*, 13 August 1971

The leaflet became the subject of one of the first headline stories concerning the festival to be taken up by the national press. They were already aware of an event that could rapidly become very newsworthy, and, as reported by a number of nationals, the local parish council advising residents of a small English village to 'lock up their gnomes' was extraordinary. Over the following days, the Weeley Festival would continue to be the subject of front-page news in every major daily and Sunday newspaper.

**The working plan.**

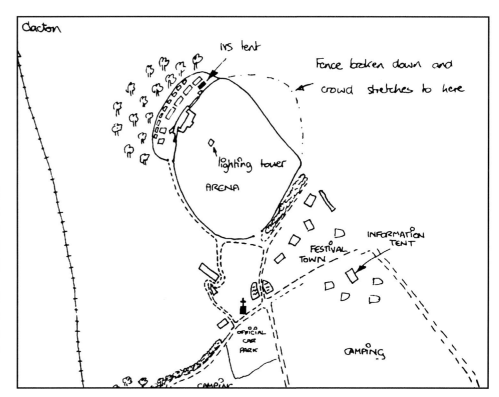

The monthly parish council meeting for August was well attended, with concerns voiced by a number of local residents and councillors. Crucially, there were still many unanswered issues. The meeting agreed to ask for more police patrols through the village in the days leading up to the festival. Major General Piggot complained that, as far as he could see, the county council were taking no steps to enforce the planning conditions agreed. The chief constable of Essex, John Nightingale, visited the site on 21 August and spoke with landowner and licensee Roger Weeley, pressing him for a detailed explanation of the security arrangements for the site, but he appeared to be ignorant of the details. Nightingale reported:

I saw Mr Stamford of the Round Table who was in charge of the concessionaires – catering, confectionary, cigarettes and the like. In answer to my question, he told me that the concessionaires had been advised to base their arrangements on an established audience of 50–80,000 and that an attendance of 80,000 would mean a profit of £50,000 for charity.

He is the only straightforward person connected with the organisation of the festival with whom I have dealt. This is the first time

such figures had been mentioned by a member of the Round Table.
**Chief constable's report, 21 September 1971**

The issue of security was certainly muddled, with various groups becoming involved. The Round Table reported that they had enlisted a number of volunteers to act as marshals around the site and to check and sell tickets on the gates. A group of local men from 'various backgrounds' were also drafted in, and members of several Hell's Angels chapters were expected to arrive over the weekend to assist. Colchester police received a tip-off about the expected arrival of Hell's Angels about three weeks before the event:

Vic Speck had decided on two forms of security. Taking care of backstage would be Hell's Angels; this was decided after discussions with Colin King, who had used Angels before on other smaller music festivals. Vic wanted front of house security and employed local security men – some called them the local mafia. They were local heavies, big well-built guys, bouncers, that sort of thing. They were the sort of people you wouldn't argue with.
**Dr Dick Farrow, Clacton GP and Clacton Round Table**

Vic brought in some local heavies; I would have objected to them had I known, as they were the dark side of Clacton. They never harmed the public, but they might have fought between themselves. I'd never been told that they'd employed them, but it was running away. I heard they'd just employed two or three of them, and their job was securing the perimeter.
**Nigel Davers, Clacton Round Table**

**The police memo warning about the Angels.** (Essex Police Museum)

I don't like security. I don't see the necessity for it. When I spoke to Vic about security, I explained, 'Once the festival was sold upfront, maybe 20-30,000 tickets, it doesn't matter, you'll have covered your costs and raised some money for charity. After that, then you don't need security – security costs a lot of money and that comes out of the money for charity.'

Once you've paid your costs, why have security? So I didn't want any security. The only security that was ever really necessary was backstage, but front-of-house security was just for people deciding they were security, and a lot of them were taking money at the door, when we'd already decided, pretty much from day one, that the gates were going to be opened free, as we'd already taken the money upfront.

**The stage takes shape, overseen by landowner Roger Weeley.** (James Gray/ANL/Rex/Shutterstock)

The Hells Angels were there to take care of backstage security. I'd worked with them for two years on two Bath Festivals, and because they knew the bands – and also because people don't argue with them. The only security you need is for people trying to get backstage, and you only need people backstage who need to be there. The Hells Angels were good at that.
**Colin King, festival show director**

The plans for policing the event had been in preparation for some time, although everyone was aware that security was to be the sole responsibility of the Round Table; Essex and Southend-on-Sea Joint Constabulary would only step in if public order was threatened or laws were being broken. Nonetheless, all police leave had been cancelled and the entire force was put on twelve-hour shifts for the Saturday and Sunday. However, it was fast becoming evident that, although the site was licensed only for the twelve hours between 6 p.m. on Saturday until 6 a.m. on Sunday, a large number of police would need to be on standby for a much longer period.

The decision was made to set up a temporary police station and command post close to the arena, and another command post on the perimeter of the festival site. Various properties in the area were also set to become temporary police offices: any detainees would be handled in Weeley Village Hall, and the press office was to be set up in the village school. A farm cottage close to the arena was to be used as a rest area for all serving officers and overnight accommodation over the weekend for the chief constable. Assistant Chief Constable John Duke was officer-in-command for the whole event.

The logistics were difficult for the officers who were scheduled to be on duty at Weeley, as well as for the extra officers drafted in during the event. Several hundred officers needed refreshments throughout the festival – an unforeseen necessity.

**Stage security.**
(Mike Sams)

With intelligence gathered regarding possible militancy from students and those favouring a counter-culture that was often evident within gatherings of young people, the arrival of an unknown number of Hell's Angels, their reputation for trouble going before them, and the probability of an audience fifteen times bigger than originally expected, the police had to be prepared for any eventuality.

All officers had a pair of handcuffs as part of their uniform, and ten extra pairs were issued for use if necessary. Preparations were also made for more compassionate needs, and a £200 contingency fund was made available to provide for festival-goers needing money to get home.

A meeting was held between the police and British Rail on 19 August. It was decided that special trains should run from London's Liverpool Street station to the tiny Weeley station on Friday 28 August, with the last train leaving the city no later than 9.25 p.m. There would be no extra trains for return journeys on Sunday 30 August, but five trains were made available to shuttle when required. Although 10,000 tickets were confirmed as sold, it was anticipated that 30–40,000 festival-goers would travel by train.

**The Angels ride in.** (Mike Sams)

All police officers were called to attend a briefing on 24 August, where they discovered a very large number of unknown factors still surrounding the festival – not least the numbers expected. The police didn't know how many people had paid to attend, and neither did the organisers. If they did, they certainly weren't saying, and no reliable information on the last-minute details could be determined.

Water and electricity supplies were finally completed just two days before the start of the festival.

'Already about 30 fans – some from abroad – have arrived on the 32-acre site for the Weeley Festival. They have set up camps in the woods surrounding the area, and more are arriving each day,' the *East Essex Gazette* reported, before speaking to a number of those already camping on-site:

> 'We came down here early to get work as we thought there would be plenty of jobs in Clacton. The others in our camp are from all over the place. There are a couple from France who have come especially for the festival.'
> ***East Essex Gazette*, 20 August 1971**

With one day to go before the gates officially opened, great concern was raised about a possible fire hazard. With loose straw still on the fields following the harvest, a large number of 'straw igloos' were sprouting up at a rapid rate, built by the festival-goers:

> The risk of fire was painfully obvious and repeated requests to the organisers to improve the situation failed to obtain the necessary action.
> **Official site report, Essex County Council**

On much of the camping and car parking areas were piles of loose straw from fields which had been harvested but from which all the straw had not been removed. Tents were pitched and cars parked amongst this; in some cases tents, once pitched, were covered in loose straw to retain warmth. Other visitors acquired straw bales and covered them with branches from the woods; some merely laid out sleeping bags and covered them with straw. Amongst all this oil and spirit stoves were lit with little thought for fire risks.
**Police Report: Essex and Southend-on-Sea Joint Constabulary**

The crops had been harvested in that particular area, but the loose straw remained, proving to be a hazard when people wanted to cook, but useful to keep warm at night. They were just heaping up loose straw with twigs and branches that they'd pulled out of the hedge and building shelters to sleep in, so these igloos were alongside the tents.
**David Weeley, Weeley resident, son of Roger Weeley, landowner**

'The village' was now taking on the look of a small tented settlement. Besides the tents erected to house administration and medical facilities, there were also a number housing welfare groups, such as the Salvation Army, St John Ambulance, the British Red Cross, Release and the 'Jesus' tent. Others were erected ready to be used by caterers, joined by hamburger, hot dog and ice cream vendors in vans, attempting to feed the thousands that were expected. A number of the early arrivals to the camping area were already without means to buy their own food and it was soon apparent that over the weekend a free food kitchen would also be needed:

> 'One of our biggest problems is the people who will spend all their money before the festival ends. We have youngsters from the Continent who have largely spent all their money to get here.'
> **Vic Speck, Clacton Round Table, talking to reporters**

**Highly flammable straw igloos.** (PA Photos /TopFoto)

A catering company from London, known as Fine Caterers, were the main concessionaires for food. They were believed by the police to be a subsidiary of Fortes, the national catering company. Another major supplier was Minters Catering Co. from Rochester. These larger companies then sublet concessions to smaller caterers and individuals:

The ice cream concession was sold for just £50 by the Round Table and with one of the hottest weekends of year forecast; it must have been seen as a pretty good deal by the vendors.
**Dr Dick Farrow, Clacton GP and Clacton Round Table**

The soundtrack of the amateur film made by members of The Round Table during the festival mentions a total of 2,500 staff on-site, including all concessionaires, catering, administrative and medical staff. It also claims there were a total of nineteen hot dog outlets and fifteen ice cream vans on-site. Festival organiser Vic Speck told reporters that, if necessary, extra food supplies would be flown in by helicopter. No one knows if this was a real prospect.

Some local businesses, outside the festival site, were stocking up for the extra customers; others were still angry that the festival was going ahead and announced their intentions of closing up for the whole weekend. The landlord of the Black Boy public house in Weeley village was among those concerned:

'These hippies keep coming in to get their water cans filled up. The locals simply won't come in while they are here'.
***East Essex Gazette***

My husband leant some of them an old Martini pub umbrella, it was baking hot and they came without any provisions, and he gave them some blankets and a couple of old saucepans so they could boil some water ... 'cos they had their little fires, and then set everything alight, we had the fire engines going up and down there.
**Ena Wade, Weeley resident**

Building teams had been working on the main stage for some time. It appeared to be a huge structure, while it was being built in the empty field, but it looked considerably smaller once the crowds started to arrive. A skeleton of scaffold poles was first assembled with scaffold boards on the floor and tarpaulins covering the entire structure, forming a roof and a protection to the sides. A 50ft-high sound and light tower was also constructed in the centre of the arena. Loud speakers on either side of the stage were capable of producing 60,000 watts, a studio 'mixing board' was assembled and the complete audio set-up used equipment worth a staggering £30,000 in total:

**The Round Table's stylised map of the site.**

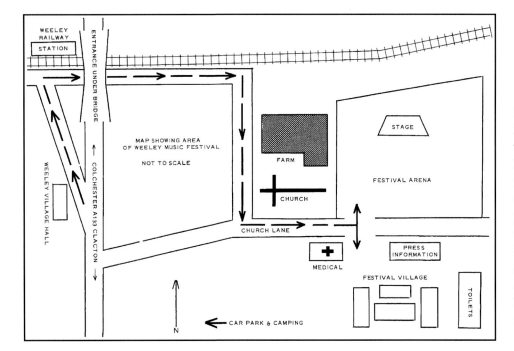

**Far out, man.** (Dick Farrow)

I was there a day before the festival started. I arrived early in my Fiat 500 with my wife to be, we had my father-in-law's huge scouting tent, with plenty of room, which we put up behind the stage. The stage itself had no resemblance … to the types of stage now; it was just a flimsy construction with canvas hanging from the roof. As for 'health and safety' there was none. It was probably life-threatening, with the wires exposed and running everywhere. Rain would have caused real problems with the wiring. I was really looking forward to an exciting weekend ahead. I'd been covering the story since it was first thought of and we were to spend the entire weekend in the backstage area mixing with the stars, in fact it became practicably impossible to get out of the back stage area.

**Mike Sams, newspaper reporter**

As the official start of the Weeley Festival of Progressive Music was just hours away, the latest editions of the music papers were once again including adverts for what *Melody Maker* billed as 'The Greatest Rock Event of The Year' – and rightly so, with a musical line-up of some of the biggest names in British music. Marc Bolan and T.Rex together with Rod Stewart and the Faces were joint top of the bill – on the posters at least; the crowd would eventually decide later who were to be the real conquerors of Weeley. Also on the bill were a mixture of well-known bands, up-and-coming artists and a selection of musicians that only the most hardened rock fans would recognise. Among the more than forty acts promised were King Crimson, Juicy Lucy, Curved Air, Mott the Hoople, Status Quo, Groundhogs, Quintessence, Rory Gallagher, Barclay James Harvest (complete with a forty-piece orchestra), Edgar Broughton, Al Stewart, Arthur Brown, Van der Graaf Generator, Principal Edwards Magic Theatre, Lindisfarne, Argent, Fairfield Parlour and of course, Mungo Jerry, the first band booked by the Round Table six months earlier.

A twelve-page programme was printed by a local newspaper and made available on-site. With a psychedelic-style colour image on the front page, the newspaper-style black-and-white pages gave brief details of many of the groups expected to attend, together with advertisements for a number of companies associated with the festival. These included record companies, pop magazines and a caterer who had booked concessions on the site. The first two pages featured a simplistic map of the site and information about the festival and its organisers.

As Friday 27 August 1971 approached, there was nothing that would prevent the Weeley Festival from going ahead. Everyone recognised that rules had already been broken, plans abandoned and potentially huge problems lay ahead, but the excitement in the air around this huge festival 'town' within a tiny Essex village was tangible:

It wasn't really until the day before the festival and we had a meeting that night, when we were then informed that the 10,000 had then increased to 20,000, perhaps even 50,000 … and we didn't really know how many were coming, but we were told that the council were having screaming hysterics and the police were warning us about traffic jams and such like and the following morning there was talk of a tailback from Chelmsford to Clacton, so what's that, 40 miles or so? I didn't get worried, but I thought, well, this is going to be a fantastic occasion, but can we handle it?

**Nigel Davers, Clacton Round Table**

The weather forecast promised a hot, dry and breezy bank holiday weekend ahead – ideal for relaxing on the coast, which was just 5 miles up the road from Weeley, but potentially hazardous for thousands of young people sitting for long hours with no respite from the sun other than flammable shelters in a tinder-box-dry field. But what a weekend this promised to be.

# A message from the organisers ...

This Festival is not 'a bread trip', every penny it makes will go to aid Bangladesh, Shelter, Release and other important charities. That means any damage done on the site, which has been given free by two local farmers, will have to be paid for out of the charity take. We feel that the best way to say thank you to the farmers for letting us have their land is to leave it the way we found it.

... And who they are
Promoters of the Pop Festival are Round Table Vice-Chairman, Vic Speck and Peter Gibbs, a past chairman.

VIC SPECK, who is 37, has been a member of the Round Table for five years. Originally from Kent, he has lived in Clacton for over 20 years and has numerous business interests in the area.

PETER GIBBS, aged 33, is a pharmacist and has also lived in Clacton for 20 years. He has been a member of the Round Table for 10 years and was its Chairman in 1969.

And why has Clacton Round Table – an organisation respected for the role it plays in business and civic life – persevered with the Festival despite intense local pressure and criticism?

'Firstly as a means of raising a considerable sum of money for charity,' Mr. Speck said, and secondly, 'because we felt that it was time this area was put on the map. But the third reason is a matter of principle. We wanted to prove that an event of this sort can be held without scenes of violence and upset,' says Mr. Speck, 'That the people who attend these festivals have a philosophy to which they are surely entitled, and that the opportunity exists for mutual understanding and respect.'

And despite the criticism and obstructions which have dogged Mr. Speck and his associates, the offers of help from both local and national organisations would seem to indicate there are many who echo these sentiments. Somewhere in an operation as immense and unpredictable as setting up a pop festival, there has to be a link man. A man whose expertise and contacts can create a sensible pattern from the chaotic elements involved.

The Clacton Round Table chanced to light on Colin King of Brighton as that man.

'It would have been impossible for us to have tackled any aspects of this event without him,' says publicity co-ordinator Norman Thompson. 'His knowledge has been invaluable to us, and the Round Table recognises that without his aid, day to day vigilance over an always changing situation, and intimate involvement in a sphere of business with its own conventions, we would have had an impossible task.'

Colin, who has been immersed in different areas of show business for the last eight years, has an ultimate ambition to stage a week long 'pop music carnival' with an audience of a million.

**Weeley Festival programme**

# 4

# THIS IS WHERE IT'S AT

The music and dancing licence for the Weeley Festival of Progressive Music was due to come into force at 6 p.m. on Saturday, but throughout Friday 27 August 1971, thousands of youngsters were making their way to a field near the coast in the small Essex village. 'The sleepy little Essex village of Weeley woke up today to a mass hippie invasion.' Reported the area's evening newspaper – the word 'hippie' was definitely the word of the moment and featured in almost every journalist's report from the festival:

Hundreds of penniless fans gathered around a free food kitchen where hippies from all over the world sat around the 'Glastonbury pot', centre of many wild hippie scenes. A goulash stew, made from food given by other hippies, boiled in an old dustbin. Visitors to the site were greeted by hippie beggars collecting money to keep the free food kitchen going.
***Southend Evening Echo*, 27 August 1971**

The *Echo* also reported about 15,000 fans an hour pouring into the village by Friday afternoon. A BBC television news crew filmed the festival site and chose to speak to one of the more mature festival fans for their evening news bulletin:

Reporter: You must be the oldest hippy here?
*Festival-goer: I'm not even a hippy, man. Don't put no labels on me. I'm not label-able, I'm an individual, man*

Do you go to all the festivals?
*Most of them, yeah*
How does this one compare with others?
*Ah, this is great, man, this is great. This is where it's all happening. This is where we recover from our summer on the road, man.*
**BBC News item**

Although special trains were due to operate during the evening, from early morning every arrival of a coast-bound train at the tiny Weeley station brought with it several hundred music fans. The A12 and the A133 trunk roads were littered with hitch-hikers, all 'thumbing a lift to Weeley. The local Colchester to Clacton bus service was inundated with festival passengers and their luggage:

At Colchester bus station, as I turned the corner, it was like a mad house, there were hundreds of people just milling around waiting for a bus, not knowing where they were going – you've got to bear in mind that they came from all parts of the county … and all parts of the country. Each passenger had a rucksack and a sleeping bag. Imagine trying to get that lot on a double-decker bus. It was chaos, absolute chaos.
**Ted Hutchings, No.19 bus driver**

In the days leading up to the festival, there had been a number of small fires in the campsite, due mainly to the very dry conditions and the amount of straw on the ground. These gave grave cause for concern, but had been beaten out quickly by those on the site before they could spread and cause injury and damage. But as the number of people flooding on to the festival fields increased, the danger intensified, as the festival-goers were bringing with them camping stoves and vehicles, and lighting campfires.

During Friday 27 August, there were at least five larger fires started and dealt with but the situation began to look more serious. The fire crew from nearby Frinton-on-Sea complained that on two occasions they had just returned to their base after fighting fires on the festival site when they had to be called back again. The festival organisers claimed, however, that a request to the Essex Fire Service to position a fire engine on-site throughout the festival had been refused. Press reports quoted a member of the organising committee:

> We'd asked Essex fire headquarters if we could have a tender on-site permanently. They said it would serve no useful purpose, so it is no good their complaining.

**At least the car parking was well organised.** (Dick Farrow)

**Feeding time at the free food kitchen.** (Getty Images)

It was a hot weekend, the crops had been cut and what was left was very dry stubble. In the early days, when the first hippies first came on-site they erected their tents and even made igloos out of straw, and if there was a fire they'd shout and all run out and jump on it and put it out.

We tried to hire, or even buy a fire engine, but were unable to. Almost opposite the festival site was Weeley fire station, but it was manned by part timers and they couldn't be there all the time. In the end we managed to get hold of some fire extinguishers and we had our own little truck and we ran around putting out fires.
**Graham Syrett, Clacton Round Table**

As it got underway we were all so busy we didn't have time for anything. We had fires, which we hadn't planned for, so suddenly we needed a fire officer, and we used my business van from Universal carpets and furniture as a fire engine.
**Nigel Davers, Clacton Round Table**

**An awful lot of people in one small space.** (*Clacton and Frinton Gazette*)

**A fire gets out of hand.**
(PA Photos/TopFoto)

**We're camped by the tree.**
(Dick Farrow)

The situation became very serious when one blaze spread through a number of tents, with a can of paraffin exploding and engulfing a motorcycle. A number of people needed medical treatment, although fortunately there were no serious injuries. The police expressed concern about the situation and regular announcements were made via the loudspeaker system from the stage advising people to take great care, to dig holes to light fires in and to keep them small. Despite the warnings, there was still a much larger blaze to come. The newspaper headlines of the next day, Saturday 28 August, told the story:

**Pop festival fans settle down in straw igloos**

**The Pop festival that burst into flames**

**Hippies flee pop festival blaze**

**Pop festival hippies flee fire in field**

As the working day came to an end, the influx of music fans making their way to the site continued. There were no reliable figures of tickets sold and rumours were rife of counterfeit tickets being available at London's Liverpool Street station, but there was no question of tickets not being available on the gate, at least at the start. Fans began arriving in their thousands and making their way to the arena hours before the start of the planned entertainment:

I travelled down by coach from Huddersfield to Clacton. As the journey progressed more and more 'hairy people' were joining the coach and I think we walked from Clacton to the site.

Although I'd been to one festival before, I still came completely unprepared for camping out in the open. I liked fishing, so I had a large fishing umbrella with me and slept under that for the first night. I used straw to sleep on, but after that I stayed in the main arena and slept where I was.
**Garry Bodenham, festival fan**

In those days, there was only one road to Clacton and it went right through Weeley, the whole area came to a standstill. I was 18 and lived in Great Clacton. My friend's mum was in the Red Cross and she was helping at the event. She was a very broad-minded person, not fazed by anything. We went with her in her Morris Oxford car and spent the whole weekend based there, sleeping in the car.
**Philip Reeve, festival fan**

I was 16, I wouldn't normally be allowed to go to festivals and concerts, they were always far away. There was no chance of going to the Isle of Wight, but Weeley was just up the road. Four or five of us went from Dovercourt, we bought the tickets from the record shop and we just slept rough. We stayed throughout the weekend; I think we were some of the first in and some of the last to leave. We found a spot where we could sit, right in front of the light tower, up against the barrier. We had a good view and there was no one behind us, but I do remember something falling off the tower, lights or something – it missed us. Interesting time – it was towards the end for some of the bands and in at the start for others, music was changing; it was a special time. There'd never been anything like it locally and never will in the future.
**Robert Day, festival fan**

I've still got my original ticket. I remember the guys on the gates were saying 'we can't deal with this', there were just so many people, so I've still got my ticket, no one took it. We set up our tent in the main arena, but decided it was too busy, so we moved and set up camp behind the stage into Weeley Wood.
**Tony Haggis, festival fan**

**The blaze gets close to 'the Village'.** (ANL/REX/ Shutterstock)

I was just 15, almost 16 and a lot of persuasion took place with my parents to allow me to go. The only reason I was allowed to go was because I'd be backstage, in a tent with Mike, now my husband, who was reporting on the whole festival. We were very lucky to be up on the stage for most of the time and we were looking out at a sea of faces. Many people put flags up to help them find where they were, because there were so many arriving all the time.

**Jeanette Sams, festival fan**

I was 16. I didn't tell the folks where I was going, it was me and a few chums, one of them was a bit older and had an old Ford Anglia. We jumped in the car and zoomed up to Weeley. We got there late Friday afternoon and things were beginning to happen by then and thousands of people were arriving, a lot of them by train, at poor little Weeley station and that was right next to the festival fields.

Anyway, we drove into the car park and there were thousands of people by the time we got there, and as a 16-year-old in my local area, I'd never

**Walking through the crowds at a music festival is never easy.** (Dick Farrow)

seen anything like it. I'd read the lists of those due to attend: T.Rex were going to be there, and King Crimson, my hero band.

It was wonderful, we were very excited about this and had a few underage beers, set up our tents and sort of gingerly looked around because we'd never seen that amount of people before, and they all had long hair ... I'd started growing my hair by then; it was an extraordinary time for everyone there. I know the Isle of Wight festival had been going for a couple of years by then, but this was certainly the biggest thing locally and I'd imagine, the biggest thing since.

It was clear that the arrangements that they'd made to cater for the number of people they were expecting were being surpassed and the facilities that they'd laid on, whether for the catering or for people sleeping in tents, were just far outweighed by the number of people there.

What a time everybody had, we didn't take much money with us, but I do remember taking a big bottle of cider which had a cork in the top.
**Tony O'Neil, festival fan**

I was at Liverpool University, so I knew all the rock bands, and used to read the magazines, like *Sounds*, *NME* and *Melody Maker* and I'd seen it advertised. I'd read about Woodstock and the Isle of Wight and I saw about this Weeley festival and thought, let's go for it.

I'd hitch-hiked all the way down from Liverpool. I came in what I stood up in; all I had with me was a haversack and a sleeping bag. I can't remember if I had food ... I got a motorbike ride for the first 50 miles or so; I'd never been on the back of a bike before. Then I got picked up by a lorry, which got a puncture about an hour later. So, I helped the driver change the wheel, and then, when we

**Appreciative fans.** (Garry Bodenham)

got into London, I helped him unload at some meat-packing firm. Then I worked my way over to Liverpool Street station, I'd never been there before. I sat on the floor by platform 18 with loads of other people.

The train came in and I got on. I hadn't a clue where Weeley was, of course. When I got off the train there were hundreds and hundreds of people heading towards these fields. I had hoped to meet up with friends. There was a guy I'd been to school with and had moved to London: didn't meet up with him, though, far too many people there. I just threw myself down, 50 yards from the stage, opened my sleeping bag, rolled in and basically,

that's all I did then – I had no tent – and then probably grabbed a hot dog.
**Trevor Davis, festival fan**

My friend Bas and I travelled on the afternoon of the first day, Friday. I think we arrived by train on Weeley station, carrying a tent, two sleeping bags and some food. We pitched our tent outside the arena and looked around. The first evening, after something to eat, we left our tent behind and went into the arena for the start of the music and the first bands up.

I recall Juicy Lucy, vaguely, but it was 3 a.m. when they were on. The music sets started at

**A quiet time at the free food kitchen.** (Dick Farrow)

'The Village' and the arena. Note Weeley church on the left. (PA Photos / TopFoto)

midnight on day one. After a while I think we gave up and went back to our tent to get some kip.

**Tim Hillyar, festival fan**

Throughout Friday afternoon and evening, records were played from the stage by a variety of people, including disc jockeys Steve Lee and David Symonds. Show organiser Colin King also turned his hand to making various announcements, many in the laid-back 'hippy' style of 'hey man …' speech that was prevalent at similar events. The records continued throughout the entire weekend, covering delays and filling the gaps while bands prepared themselves for their appearances. One of the records played was an anthem for Weeley, in the form of a chant and stomping background; it had been recorded especially for the festival. Another favourite was a record featuring the drums of the African Burundi tribe:

One track that the PA was playing between bands that I remember, and it seemed to be on all the time, was 'Riders on the Storm' by The Doors. It was just played over and over again and at that volume, in the middle of a field of hippies – what a time we had.

**Tony O'Neil, festival fan**

I remember records being played between acts, in particular the triple album of Woodstock … this included announcements from the original concert, so they sounded a bit confusing when hearing them from the stage at Weeley. The Doors' *LA Woman* album was played too, oh, and 'Riders on the Storm'.

**Garry Bodenham, festival fan**

The residents of Weeley were bemused by the whole thing. Many had voiced their fears of an invasion by 'wild hippies', but they had really only formed these opinions based on what they had seen on television and read in newspapers. Obviously there were a number of villagers who had already made up their minds that these were going to be 'bad people', but many were surprised and quickly came to recognise the vast majority of the festival fans as normal, polite, well-behaved youngsters – even if many of them did have long hair. Not many hippies had ever visited Weeley before, or since, so they hadn't really known what to expect.

Weeley residents were not only coming to terms with the thousands of festival fans, but also with the village being inundated by newspaper, TV and radio reporters and journalists:

Most people in the village are co-operating with the fans. They show no resentment to them and generally find them to be decent, respectable young people. It seems to me there exists an air of comradeship between the fans and villagers that existed during the war.

We expected the worst, but they've turned out to be very well behaved indeed.

They all say 'please' and 'thank you'. I don't think they could be more courteous.

*Colchester Gazette*, **27 August 1971**

The people of Weeley didn't know what had hit them. They were expecting a lot of people, but there were crowds of people. They came off the tiny Weeley station. Many arrived by car or they hitchhiked in, and they were buying up food as they went through the village. The shops just emptied, the shelves were just cleared, cigarettes especially, drink… I don't know how they coped.

**Mike Sams, newspaper reporter**

The village was swamped. My father, who was the baker then, didn't go to bed all weekend. He stayed up for the whole three days, just baking, and the shop was open more or less twenty-four hours a

day. He used to say he took a year's takings in a weekend, I think he'd have wanted it to happen every year – people were coming round to the shop all the way through the night.

We ended up looking after a lot of valuables in the shop. Fans would come into the shop and buy cakes and bread and then come back and say, 'Could you look after these for us?' Jewellery, money ... my mother would put it in an envelope and lock them away, write their name on it for them to collect it later.

**Hoss Selfe, Weeley resident, baker and musician**

The shops ran out of food. We used to have Morrison's the paper shop, that's now closed, and the post office, and there were just queues and queues ... and the other thing was the telephone box. They queued up at the telephone box every evening to ring home to tell their parents they'd arrived safely.

All the shops looked after the locals and made sure we had stuff ... and the baker still does, saves my loaf of bread on a Saturday and makes sure it doesn't go to strangers.

**Renee Marshall, Weeley resident**

**Weeley Festival's water supply.** (Dick Farrow)

During that time I found that there was a good atmosphere all around the village and a rapport with people, they were all polite. My mum, who was 73, lived up Weeley Street. They used to go up the pub, but they drank that dry. Mum used to say, 'What nice boys and girls they are.' She'd say to my husband, 'Take us over the pop field, Bob.' She loved it over there.
**Ena Wade, Weeley resident**

I was only 10 or 11. My dad ran Hillside Garage in the village. We had a load of scrap cars out the

**The free food 'kitchen'.**
(Dick Farrow)

back and some of them from the festival slept in them. I remember we had an outside toilet too and they were queuing, about fourteen deep, to have a wash and brush up, but it was all very peaceful.
**Cliff Mason, Weeley resident**

I'd never, ever seen so many people in my life. It started on the Friday, and our road was absolutely full of cars; they were parked everywhere, yet we hadn't heard a sound. We had choir practice up at the church on the Friday night and as we went home it was like fairyland with all the lights and little campfires in front of the tents. It looked like a biblical scene.
**Pearl Byford, Weeley resident and current churchwarden**

As nightfall approached, the arena and festival site took on an amazing appearance. There were tents of all shapes and colours, together with erratically built shelters made from plastic sheeting. Many were illuminated by small portable gaslights and cookers. Flags or banners fluttered in the cool evening air, tied to branches gathered from the adjacent woodland, to help identify where possessions had been left, and thousands of chilled-out youngsters relaxed and reclined around it all. Recorded music was played from the stage when the bands were not entertaining the crowds, and the mood was very relaxed and peaceful.

But there was one major cause for concern for the thousands sitting in the main arena: at this time it was a normal practice for farmers to burn the straw and stubble on their fields after harvest; it was usually done in the evening. This was something that had not been done on the festival site, as there had not been time, but was still taking place in adjacent fields and although the site looked strangely beautiful, with entire fields ablaze over-shadowing the trees and buildings, including Weeley church, it appeared very

threatening for those sitting in the arena field who were not aware of some rural practices, and many became very nervous.

Hey man, don't worry about the flames, they won't hurt you – it's just the farmer burning his fields
**Stage announcement**

Although more than forty bands were scheduled to appear at Weeley, it was a local resident who kicked off proceedings, heralding the start of more than sixty hours of music: An impromptu accordion recital was performed by Clacton pensioner 'Pop' Sherman. The bemused crowd were not sure if this was part of the show or a sound test, but treated him to rapturous applause, and then, at midnight, the first bona fide act of the festival made their way to the stage. Hackensack was the band given the honour, or perhaps having the misfortune, to be first up.

It was a difficult task to entertain a transient crowd, many of whom had been travelling all day and would probably have benefited from sleep before the show really started. But the music continued through the early hours of Saturday and into the daylight hours. At 4.45 a.m. the Edgar Broughton Band took to the stage, and despite the early hour managed to wake the crowd enough to earn an encore:

It turned out to be a much bigger event than any of us expected it would be. We thought we were going to some tiny little festival, like on a cricket ground or something like that, and as I recollect … Weeley stared out as a kind of 'free festival' idea, very underground, that sort of grew. It was huge.
**Rob Broughton, Edgar Broughton Band**

In the years since their appearance at Weeley, Status Quo have enjoyed huge success. As day broke on the Saturday morning of the Weeley festival they were next to go on stage:

**They came from far and wide.** (Dick Farrow)

The main problem with that festival was getting there. I remember it was just mayhem all around the roads about there.

I think we were supposed to be on at something like one or two in the morning, back then those 'all-nighters' just kept going, which was kinda silly. The thing I mainly remember is that Edgar Broughton were on and one of their songs kept going on and on. I remember it being really odd ... 'Out demons out' ... and I thought, well, how much bloody longer can you keep telling 'em to get out ... I never understood what they were on about at the time, but it was just a mess. Everything was over running and, when we went on, it was just

**The first act on stage, 'Pop' Sherman and his accordion, kicks off the festival.**

as everyone was asleep, just this whole mass of people, I don't know how many ... but they were all really asleep.

I had a massive split in my jeans, they'd actually split from the seam. I thought I was being wild with me leg hanging out and as we came off, our manager's partner was standing there saying, 'Go back on ... you've got an encore, get back on ...' and we said, 'we know what we're doing.'

Everyone credited us as breaking out at the Reading festival, but it was more to do with the Weeley festival ... I'm kinda glad that we've come forward in that respect. Things are far more organised than they were then.
**Francis Rossi, Status Quo**

Although the festival traffic had been heavy throughout Friday, it reached a peak between 2 a.m. and 5 a.m. on Saturday morning, according to the official police report; many thousands entered the area during this time. The queues were such that people were parking along the verges on the approach to Weeley and setting up camp on the side of the road. This issue had not been anticipated during the planning stage, and for several hours there was delay and confusion while roadside campers were woken and moved on, and extra space for parking was found.

I remember seeing Weeley station; there were so many people that the trains couldn't get in because of all the crowds, all the roads and grass verges were chock-a-block with cars. The assistant chief constable brought tow wagons down and ... anything left on the grass verge after a certain time was going to be towed away. An announcement saying this was made over the public address.
**Brian Simpson, police officer**

According to the police, the answer was to open up fields that belonged to the neighbouring farmer,

Bill Leiper. He'd met with the police on at least two occasions before the festival and explained that just because part of his land was shown on the plan of the festival site; it didn't mean that he'd given his permission for its use:

Parking and the cars were a problem, there were just too many people, and of course, we weren't expecting them all, and we had to make quick decisions about what we were going to do to get them off the road. The police were pushing for a decision to be made and I believe the car parking on the road went back many miles, many miles.

The owner of the main site was Roger Weeley, but the next door farmer was a chap named Bill Leiper, it was his land that we had to take liberties on

**A lot of people in a small space on a very hot day.**
(Dick Farrow)

**The lighting gantry looks precarious.** (Getty Images)

and open up for car parking. We had to make the decision without his knowledge and without his approval. He wasn't at all happy at that happening – but we had little choice, we were being pushed by the police to sort out the parking problems. Having said that, I know that he, as a farmer, he'd been having aggro for a while, as he was trying to do his job, with hippies coming on to the site two or three weeks beforehand and getting in his way. He did have a lot of aggravation.
**Graham Syrett, Clacton Round Table**

This farmer was going bananas, because when the traffic queues had got so bad, a police inspector came to me and told me to knock down the hedge and let in more traffic, but then the owner came along and said, 'You can't do that.'
**Nigel Davers, Clacton Round Table**

The makeshift facilities that had been constructed on the site during the previous week or so, were now being put to the test, as the numbers on the festival site started to match the population of a large town.

Sooner or later everyone attending Weeley festival had to use the toilets:

The toilet facilities certainly left a lot to be desired, especially the gents. I remember it being a long trench with an A-framed scaffold at each end and a rusty pole in between, over which one could hang … if desired! By the Sunday evening you can image that it was quite extraordinary. They had given the ladies some privacy; I seem to remember a sort of flapping curtain sort of hanging around. But for the guys … I remember standing there trying to be very private amongst hundreds of other people all in a row …

Well, the guy right next to me and my mate … he looked in a bit of a poor way; he was just half asleep and rocking backwards and forwards on this pole. He had his rucksack on … and a sleeping bag, bedroll on the back; he just went backwards and he fell backwards into the trench, I remember it well. I think I just made off and walked away. I don't remember what happened to him, he must have been assisted out, but I do remember his bedroll going by, and I do remember it was, shall we say, christened by everyone as it went by.

They certainly weren't the best facilities, but I don't think anyone really complained, because they couldn't; I mean, what a line-up of bands!
**Tony O'Neil, festival fan**

I remember the toilets. They were just long trenches with a long canvas around them. There was no privacy there at all and the women's were just like squares of canvas, but only about 3ft high.
**Tony Haggis, festival fan**

The toilets were a big hole in the ground with a bit of canvas around them – I didn't pay much attention to them, you didn't have to, your senses would have told you where they were.
**David Weeley, Weeley resident, son of Roger Weeley, landowner**

Once or twice, when I had to go to the loo, you'd look down the line, as you do, and there'd be some poor devil perched… not a pretty sight and certainly not acceptable nowadays… and if anyone lost their wallet I think it stayed in there.
**Graham Syrett, Clacton Round Table**

The toilets! I didn't want to use them, I just held on I think – that's probably why I didn't eat or drink much, and I just lay there … I calculate I was there for sixty hours or so. The weather must have been good, cos' I don't remember getting wet, I had a sort

**130,000 people viewed from the air. Can you see Wally?** (*Sunday Telegraph*)

of dark yellow corduroy suit that I wore in those days. I'd never really been away from Liverpool before, it was just a really great adventure. I was only 19.
**Terry Davis, festival fan**

The public toilets were dreadful – and certainly not a place you'd go to until it was absolutely necessary. The facilities back stage were, perhaps, slightly better, if only because they weren't being used by over 100,000 people. We were okay behind the stage. The lavatories, for the majority, were little more than trenches and there were several reports of people falling in, it was just a dug trench and people just had to do their best, so to speak.
**Mike Sams, newspaper reporter**

I was a bit spoilt; I had my own caravan back stage and my own toilets. I did visit the public toilets on one occasion and nearly died, they were absolutely disgusting. But then saying that, so are boy scouts' toilets at a camp. So if you're going out camping in the countryside, that's what happens, you get a trench, but I suppose if you get a hundred thousand boy scouts, it's not the same is it?
**Colin King, festival show director**

I'd never been in such bad loos in my whole life, or ever since, thank goodness, and these were the artist's ones. I don't know what the others were like, but it was just absolutely disgusting. And being hot ... I won't go on!
**Julie Felix, performer**

While the design of the toilets was lacking in quality and basic sanitation, the medical facilities were very well equipped and able to handle all medical emergencies. Local GP and Round Table member Dr Dick Farrow had taken on the role of medical officer for the festival and, understandably, was taking the task

very seriously. He and his team of fellow doctors and nurses, together with medics from volunteer organisations, were kept busy, with more than 250 patients seen during Friday night alone:

When I said 'yes' to providing a little first-aid cover, I hadn't realised that eight months later I would be providing a major health centre at Weeley, fully staffed and fully equipped, and dealing with hundreds of patients. One of the problems I had was that nothing had been recorded or written about what was required for such an event. I was working from virgin territory, really. There were no records or any material anywhere as to what was required at such an event.

'The Village.' (Mike Sams)

So I had to write to drug companies. I saw all the drug reps that came to the Clacton surgery and asked them if I could have equipment and medications to equip the temporary centre. The other problem was the festival was to be held on an August bank holiday. The local hospital in Clacton was then staffed by GPs like myself, so I had difficulty in getting a rota together, but I did manage, eventually, to get eleven local GPs to form part of a rota, with two senior officers of the St John Ambulance Association, and we happened to have a dentist who was a member of Round Table which was useful. We also had a vet! We were also able to call upon seventy-five members of the St John Ambulance, nineteen members of the British Red Cross and four local state registered nurses from the hospital. So we'd managed to build up a rota for the three days of the festival.

One of the things I was determined to do was, because there had been no previous records, was to try and collate some statistics from the pop festival, and three of my secretaries did a rota for the seventy-two hours, from the Friday morning to the Monday morning, and they were able to register every patient that came into the health centre. Overall there were 1,700 people seen in that seventy-two-hour period, and, as you can imagine, they covered everything that an ordinary accident and emergency department at a major hospital would cover.

Well of course there were a lot of minor problems, but one of the problems with Weeley was that it was extremely hot ... In those days people were not so conscious of sunburn, for example, so we had cases of sunburn, cases of dehydration, because a lot of the young people were in the arena for many, many hours at a time and they were not getting out to rehydrate themselves, and that led to other medical problems.

**Dr Dick Farrow, Clacton GP and Clacton Round Table**

With thousands entering the festival site, the gatekeepers were overwhelmed; they were made up of Round Table members and volunteer helpers. Although many tickets had been prepaid and sent out to the buyers, no opportunity was lost on selling more on the gate, at least that was the plan, the financial success of the festival and the ability for the bills to be paid and the charities to benefit, was solely dependent on ticket sales:

The security firm that were to collect the money from the gates refused to provide any trucks unless we paid in advance. So there was me and one of our Round Table members, Neil, and he was one of the most honest men I knew. The two of us were taking the money as all these people were coming in and the bags became full, as nobody came to collect the money, we were stuffing the cash into these holdalls that we had and they became full. Neil said, 'What do I do?' so I told him to zip his jacket up and put your belt round the bottom and stuff the money into your jacket and then we can offload it when someone eventually comes. After about two hours we both looked like Michelin men and could get no more money in and we didn't want to move because the cars would just drive in without paying.

We finally got someone, Tiny Singleton, to come along with some sacks in his old Mercedes with a huge boot, so we unloaded all these notes into the boot of his car, there must have been £15,000 to £20,000 there. He shut the boot and went off and then two hours later he had to come back and do it again. We could have been mugged; I'd never seen so much money in my life. Now as the security firm refused to come out we couldn't get to the bank until after the bank holiday. Eventually, I think, we had over £100,000 in bags, which we put it in someone's cellar and two of us slept there until we could get it to the bank!

**Nigel Davers, Clacton Round Table**

The official police report that was written after the festival gave an insight into the number of music fans on the site during the festival period:

> It is impossible to say precisely how many were on the site. The organisers do not know – or will not say – how many persons paid for admission. One estimate is that on Saturday morning there were 100,000 people there and this number certainly continued to increase throughout Saturday and Sunday morning.
>
> All visitors appeared happy and good-tempered and were extremely well behaved. There was no evidence of hostility to police officers and many youngsters were very friendly.
> **Weeley Festival police report**

It had been agreed that the majority of police officers would be kept in the background, unless called for to maintain order in the main public area. The officer in charge was the assistant chief constable of Essex, John Duke, but also present for most of the weekend was the county's chief constable, John Nightingale. Officers were seconded to Weeley from all over the county, and it's probably fair to say, that many of them, especially from the rural areas of Essex, had never seen so many people in one place before:

> A few men were stationed on duty on the right of way running through the area. The number of officers in uniform visible within the area was kept to a minimum. There were reserves available, but were kept out of sight of the crowds.
>
> Extensive radio communications were provided and the production manager of the festival, Colin King, who was in charge of the stage, was allowed the use of a police pocket radio to pass information or call for assistance if necessary.
> **Weeley Festival police report**

PC John Newbury was still in his first year as a police constable and spent time on duty at the festival:

> We were deployed from Basildon in the old blue transits that we had in those days, with bench seats down the sides. When we got there we were stationed in one of the farm workers houses, it was obviously empty at the time. The upstairs was occupied by the chief constable and he was a real down to earth, feet on the ground chief constable. I remember him, it was a hot August evening and he was wandering around, pair of shorts, bare chested - you wouldn't see chief constables doing that nowadays, but that was him, he was approachable, he was there, he was with his blokes and girls, doing the job that we were sent to do.
>
> My recollections are that it was very laid-back, it was enjoyable, everyone enjoyed it, the police officers that were there enjoyed it, certainly on the nightshift, I don't know about the day, I think they had their problems, but it wasn't intimidating, it wasn't threatening; it just felt quite comfortable walking around
> **John Newbury, police officer**

> We were 'weekend off' that weekend and it was a case of 'anyone want any overtime?' Well you jumped at it in those days and that's what we did, we all volunteered to go down there for the Friday, Saturday and Sunday.
>
> We were told we were going to a music festival. There was no idea of the numbers of people that were expected; they didn't have the intelligence system that they have now. Nobody was warned how many were coming, and then we heard that special trains were being put on from Liverpool Street station – that was quite a thing in those days.
>
> We were told just to patrol and watch out for petty thieving, just general police patrol work – that's all we were told. I've been on operations since,

but in those days there was no proper briefing. There were police drafted in from most divisions throughout Essex and we were just dumped down there in pairs and told to walk round the ground – we were walking around at night-time, I just about saw it as day broke and the music was still blaring out as I recall, it was playing all night. I don't recall it ever going quiet.

We were based in the old vicarage in Weeley; that became our central post and that's where we operated from. We had a static base and a place where we took our refreshments from.

The fans certainly weren't aggressive to us. The people were singing and they were happy; they were out to have a good time. I think we were told to look the other way 'cos I don't think we had the facilities to handle it. I don't recall many people being arrested, not the regular festival people anyway, there were perhaps some arrests in the daytime and possibly some drunks too, but certainly at night-time and at four o'clock in the morning, we were walking around the arena and there were only eight or ten of us on duty for the second half of the night and we were told 'don't take too many prisoners'.

**Brian Simpson, police officer**

# 5

# FAR OUT, MAN

Although there was a low visible police presence of uniformed officers, members of a drugs team were on-site and patrolled the whole festival grounds. It would have been naive to think that drugs wouldn't be available and a potential problem at the festival, and so, besides specialist police officers, the medical team, backed up by the drugs charity Release, were prepared. But there can be no denying that August 1971, was a far more innocent time than now:

Tiny, another of the Round Table members came into medical centre on the Friday evening and asked me to walk around the site with him. I'd been working through the day and he suggested that I take a break. Well, what I saw I will never forget, there were just so many tents and flags and colours.

I remember saying, perhaps naively, 'What's that smell?' 'That's hash' he replied. Three days later I was the world's expert on drugs!
**Dr Dick Farrow, Clacton GP and Clacton Round Table**

There were people selling various things about; I didn't indulge in anything like that.
**Terry Davis, festival fan**

My husband, Bob, was over there having a look with our village policeman one evening. They were talking and Bob was rolling an old Golden Virginia cigarette, this man came up and said, 'Man, would you like a joint?'

David, our policeman said, 'that's the wrong flavour for me mate.'
**Ena Wade, Weeley resident**

It was the first time I'd smelt or seen anything to do with drugs, I was a bit naive about drugs in those days, there wasn't so much of it about. It was the first time that I'd smelt that sickly sweet smell and seen people just gazing.
**Brian Simpson, police officer**

There were people with small amounts of drugs mainly for personal use, the favourite place for hiding it in those days was in their underwear usually. In those days you could detect users more easily than you can now; they used to cover themselves with a particular oil to cover up the smell of cannabis – I think it was called patchouli oil. They might have just smelled of cannabis because it was indicative of what was going on.
**Unnamed police officer**

We were walking around and observing, if we saw any drugs changing hands, we wouldn't make a move there and then. It would have been us against a whole load of people and they'd all have turned on us and we'd have lost our man, so we'd keep an eye on them and follow them when they

moved. Everyone has to go to the toilets eventually. So when they were alone, away from the groups, then that's when we'd stop them.
**Peter Whent, police officer**

The drugs officers were arresting people for passing drugs and I had to take drug samples from Weeley, by motorcycle, to the Elephant and Castle in London to have them sampled, then I had to bring back the results … it's about 70 miles each way, and I did that all weekend, right through the night.
**Unnamed police motorcyclist**

Yes there were quite a few substances around. There was a tent that was run by Release [Independent drugs awareness charity]. They were looking after people who were using drugs and had bad experiences, and there were also some local doctors there. They all did a wonderful job.

I still remember going to the tent and the doctors saying to me, 'There are people having bad acid trips'; they were jabbering idiots really. There was one man who'd actually fallen in the toilets and was completely out of it and he looked a real mess – and Release had a really good method of bringing people back from bad trips, because you'd think they'd just say 'There, there … you'll be OK …', but that doesn't work, because they're so far off their heads they don't understand that. What they had was a box of jam and cream doughnuts and they'd just pick one out and squash it in their face, and down from the trip they came - into the world of jam and cream. It was great and seemed to work a treat and off back into the festival they'd go, and then probably took more drugs and came back later on. It was days of experimentation, no one really knew. The newspapers were full of people taking LSD and trying to fly … I didn't see anyone like that.
**Colin King, festival show director**

There were tents housing drugs organisations. I don't think drugs were a big problem, but there were specialist people there. I personally didn't see any sign of drugs, but there were a lot of joss sticks around, and if you get that many people in the same place then you get a particular smell from them anyway; there was a funny smell all over the place of course.
**Graham Syrett, Clacton Round Table**

There certainly were drugs there; we were at the height of the flower power time. We had arranged for an organisation known as Release to come down from London, they were a voluntary organisation, consisting of physiatrists, psychiatric nurses, psychologists and also solicitors. They had a large tent and their policy was to decorate, if you like, this tent with rugs and quiet music and incense, and anybody who was under the influence of, say, LSD, or tripping, would be brought in, they would be assigned to a carer who would then calm them down, rehydrate them and try to get them to sleep through the problem.

Sadly, of course, they were overwhelmed very quickly and I had to take the overflow into the medical centre; we weren't able to follow that policy but we were able to give them injections to calm them down and give them a good sleep for a few hours and then send them on their way.

One of the problems that we did have with LSD was that some of it carried some impurities and we had one or two difficult medical cases causing, for example, epilepsy, and these had to be sent to Colchester hospital. Clacton hospital, which was nearer, was busy dealing with all the tourists coming down for the bank holiday, and so I couldn't use that, and I was asked by Colchester only to send the more severe cases, which we did.
**Dr Dick Farrow, Clacton GP and Clacton Round Table**

# 6

# ANGELS OR DEMONS?

Prior to the start of the festival, and throughout Friday, a number of Hell's Angels had started to assemble on-site. A few of them had been involved in building fences, while the site was in the construction stage, but as more arrived, they were allocated other jobs: patrolling arena fences, assisting on the gate, backstage security and firefighting:

> Well, anyone who lived through that era would know that the Hell's Angels were the self-appointed security forces of pop festivals and any other big events, and whenever one was held they would turn up and they would expect to be given the remit to look after security. It wasn't a question of being invited at all.
> **Mike Sams, newspaper reporter**

During Friday, the Angels already on-site had assisted firefighters and festival organisers in containing the straw fires that erupted on the campsite:

> We were told we had to walk around in twos, for safety reasons, but there were no problems we never had any hassle with anybody. We did have Hell's Angels come down and enjoy themselves, but we had no trouble at all with them. They did actually help us once or twice, we had to use water from the pond near the church, it had quite a bit of water in it and we had to put our pump in there.

> These Hell's Angels were good, they used to jump in and put the hose in and then we'd take up the water. Cor, it didn't half honk down there!
> **Alec Gibbs, Weeley fireman**

There were groups of the bikers from various parts of the UK, most of them members of Hell's Angels chapters and many areas were represented: Cotswold Chapter from Cheltenham, Diablos Chapter from Bournemouth, Druids Chapter from Southampton, the local Essex Chapter, Freewheelers Chapter from Aldershot and Reading, Nomads Chapter from East London, West Country Chapter from Bristol and the Wolverhampton Chapter from the Midlands. Other smaller groups of motorcyclists also made their way to the site; they, too, made their way to the backstage area assuming a security role:

> There seemed to be a lot of Hell Angels everywhere with rows and rows of their bikes parked up at the edge of the field. I later learned these were the marshals – the event security team!
> **Tim Hillyar, festival fan**

More Hell's Angels were arriving on-site during Saturday morning, riding through the village in a pack on their flashy customised machines, many with 'Easy Rider'-style handlebars and highly polished chrome exhausts. One machine had a fuel tank shaped like a coffin! Wherever they went they

**Police escort a Hell's Angel from the site.** (ANL/REX/Shutterstock)

were noticed, and enjoyed putting on a show. To many members of the public they were seen as a threatening, unlawful mob, with long, greasy hair and unwashed denim and leather clothing.

The Weeley villagers were taking in all the many unusual and amazing sights that had engulfed their village, the arrival of the Hell's Angels was just another spectacle that nobody had ever expected to see, riding in convoy past their garden gates.

It was going really well, and then the Hell's Angels turned up. They came up that Weeley Hill, and my two neighbours – both were well into their sixties – used to hang over their gates with their arms folded, and one said 'Oh, look here come those Hell's Angels … we'll have to lock ourselves away they'll rape us' and they went flying indoors!
**Ena Wade, Weeley resident**

Not all the Hell's Angels arrived by motorcycle, and not all Hell's Angels were equal, especially the newly initiated; within their ranks they had their own hierarchy. Tony Stacey from Essex was known as 'The Prof' and together with his fellow Angels, arrived in Weeley on Saturday morning:

We went up there, half a dozen of us. We were a newly formed chapter in the Essex region, affiliated to 'The Bastards' from Coggeshall and we were from Billericay. We were new at the time and we

**Hell's Angels are dragged from the jeeps.** (Mike Sams)

**The caterers' security team.** (ANL/REX/Shutterstock)

turned up at the pop festival in a van, six of us. As we arrived at the gate we were told, 'Oh, you're Hell's Angels, you're security, come on in. The beer tent is behind the stage.' So we thought, 'yeah, great stuff, we'll have some of this.'

So there we are, in the beer tent – we're security, in the beer tent, this is fantastic – and then in walked another chapter of Hell's Angels. And these were real Hell's Angels from the Wessex Chapter. We sort of eyed each other up and down, chatted a bit and then I noticed my vice-president was missing: Tramp, Dougie. I asked where he'd gone and someone said he'd gone out the back to 'fight for his colours'.

The next thing I know, there's another group from Wolverhampton walked in and by now we were rather outnumbered, and it was, 'Hand your colours over, or else.' At this particular juncture, being only five of us now, we didn't have much of an option, so our colours got handed over and we were unceremoniously booted out of the beer tent.

Round the front of the stage, after we'd got out, we noticed that Dougie was still missing, so I said to the others, 'Well I'm going to go round the back to find him.' The rest said, 'What?' and I replied, 'Well there's only one guy on the gate.' So I went back, told him what had happened and he said, 'No, there's been no fights round here,' so

**Strange collaboration: a police officer gets a lift.** (PA Photos/TopFoto)

I started to 'give it the large one', when another four or five of them appeared from behind this fence – and I'm sure the name David Hawkes rings a bell, [Dave Hawkes was well known within Hell's Angels circles. A former police cadet, he became a spokesman for the Angels during the ensuing court cases.] I can't remember if he was with the Wolverhampton Angels or from the Wessex Freewheelers – anyway, he came to the fore and told me in no uncertain terms that I shouldn't be there. Well, once you start the bravado you can't really back down, so I didn't, whereupon a head hit me on the nose. At which point I whistled, turned around and calmly walked off.

We went back to the van that we'd arrived in and as we opened the back door we were very nearly set upon by Dougie, Tramp. He'd been waiting there with a wrench in his hand. I did say to the guys after a while let's go back in – the rest of the chapter from Coggeshall were going to be turning up later in the afternoon – but they really decided they'd had enough for the day so we left. It was only afterwards that we found that the Coggeshall Bastards did turn up later, about seventy strong, which would have made quite a bit of difference, and apparently did make a difference because they were welcomed with opened arms.

Our intention was to go and listen to the music. We didn't go there looking for trouble. We had no problem with the Hippies, but in the end we didn't get to see any of the concert and we didn't do any security. We just sampled the payment – for a while.
**Tony Stacey, Hell's Angel**

Although many of those at the festival were aware of the Hell's Angels' presence, they'd had little contact with them. There had been scuffles between the Angels themselves and, according to them it was how they enjoyed themselves. Round Table member Graham Syrett witnessed one incident, on the Saturday morning, that caused him concern:

I saw first-hand the distortion of the story by some of the press, the reporting was so totally way out in some papers. I actually witnessed them paying Hell's Angels to fight so they could photograph them and put them on the front page of the paper to make big headlines and over exaggerate the particular problem that we had.
**Graham Syrett, Clacton Round Table**

There were a few public appearances by the Angels. Surprisingly perhaps, very few audio recordings survive of the festival, but a recording of one of the Angels addressing the crowds from the stage does exist:

We don't want no bother, but if they want it we're gonna give it to them, we're gonna give it to everybody – so you either want us or you don't … now let's have it, which way do you f***ing want it, I want an answer, yes or no ?
**Unknown Hell's Angel**

The response from the arena was a resounding 'No'.

But, while the music continued from the stage, with the crowds either enjoying the music or attempting to sleep through it, out of view several clashes involving the Hell's Angels were taking place. Around midmorning, most of the Hell's Angels had congregated behind the stage and were drinking heavily; they had a reputation for helping themselves to whatever they wanted at previous festivals, though whether they'd helped themselves or were freely offered the beer in this instance is unclear:

The angels … just rode in. I think there were two chapters, maybe more and somebody said to pacify them, 'give them some beer'. It was the worst possible thing that could happen.
**Nigel Davers, Clacton Round Table**

Nonetheless, there was 'a history' between some of the concessionaires and the Angels, and consequently a

☛ **Went there, had the t-shirt.** (Dick Farrow)

➥ **Straw and a gas
stove – a risky
combination.**
(Dick Farrow)

**This way to the ladies'.** (Dick Farrow)

**A straw settlement: home at Weeley.** (Dick Farrow)

**Collecting straw for the igloos.** (Dick Farrow)

↰ Are you sitting
comfortably? The
ladies' toilets. (Dick
Farrow)

← **Putting the finishing touches to the stage.** (Dick Farrow)

↓ **Backstage before the show.** (Dick Farrow)

t **Home is where your car is.** (Garry Bodenham)

ↆ **Walking towards the church from the campsite.** (Garry Bodenham)

**← Rod Stewart and the Faces.** (Garry Bodenham)

**↓ Dusk approaches .. or is it dawn?** (Garry Bodenham)

**◄ The music was non-stop.** (Garry Bodenham)

**► The arena, and the village to the left.** (Dick Farrow)

**◄ Flags at festivals are not new.** (Garry Bodenham)

t **One of many fires during the weekend.**
(Dick Farrow)

☛ Marc Bolan with
wife June and the bus.
(David Dagley/REX/
Shutterstock)

**↑ View from St Andrews church tower of the arena.**
(Derrick Byford)

**↜ Same view in 2016.**
(June Deville)

↲ **View from St Andrews church tower of the camping area.** (Derrick Byford)

↰ **Same view in 2016.**

t A view of the arena
from the backstage area.
(Hoss Selfe)

**Local band Mustard.** (Hoss Selfe)

**Backstage during the festival.** (Hoss Selfe)

↑ **Police on the scene after trouble between the Angels and security.** (Kevin Herridge)

↓ **Tension mounts with the Angels.** (Kevin Herridge)

← **Some chose to camp in the arena. The stage is visible in the distance.** (Dick Farrow)

↓ **Cover of the official programme.**

WEELEY
5p
FESTIVAL OF
PROGRESSIVE MUSIC.

**Police restrain one of the fighters.** (ANL/REX/ Shutterstock)

number of clashes occurred, with the Angels making demands for food, drink or money.

It was difficult to know if members from all the various chapters were involved, as some still claimed that they were employed on security and firefighting tasks, but at around 11 a.m. a major disturbance broke out in a marquee in 'the village'. One report suggests the trouble started with an Angel taking cans of Coca-Cola; some versions of this story suggest a whole stall was overturned. Fine Caterers Ltd of Battersea claimed that staff were threatened, and ovens and a catering unit were wrecked by the Angels. The police said they were not aware, at the time, of this incident. As it had been agreed that they would play no part in festival security unless they were notified of trouble, this was probably so. However, the caterers were not happy with what they saw as a complete lack of proper security arrangements provided by the Round Table, so they took steps to make their own arrangements for security and calls went out for assistance. Precisely what happened next will probably never be known. A number of different factions and individuals were involved, and each has their own story of how things evolved. As such, some aspects of what exactly happened and when are unclear:

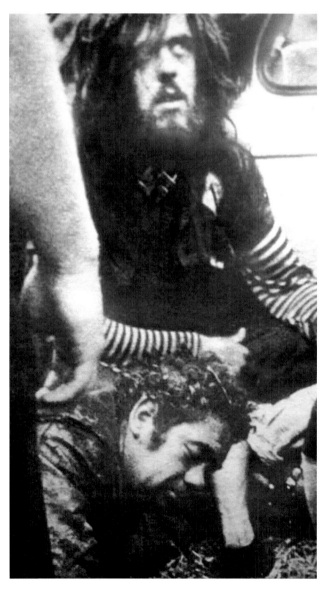

**Injured Angels.** (Mike Sams)

I was in the food tent where one of the caterers had their counter and everybody was queueing happily and smiling even though there were long queues to buy milk and bread, Coca-Cola, that sort of thing, and then suddenly this Hell's Angel just drove straight the way through the whole crowd, knocking some people over, and one of them was a young girl, about 16. She wasn't badly injured but she was knocked on her back, so her boyfriend shouted at this Hell's Angel, who then got off his bike and started beating this chap up, who was not aggressive in any way.

I jumped in to get there, but he'd got on his bike and ridden off. I decided then that we had to stop them, so I called up the man in charge of the police, the chief constable, John Nightingale, on our communications system, to say they were running riot and I needed police into the area immediately.

He said to me, 'If you think I'm going to send in forty-five officers to take on two chapters of Angels you're mistaken.' We had a few words and I said, 'Well, you've got to do something.' He said, 'Well, you've created this problem and until I get reinforcements ...' He didn't refuse to come in; he said, 'I just haven't got enough men to send in, and I won't send them in on a lost cause, I could end up with forty officers being beaten up. When I get reinforcements ...' he said. So I said, 'Well, when is that?' and he replied, 'When I get them ... I don't know.'

That's how it all started.

**Nigel Davers, Clacton Round Table**

Festival organiser Colin King, who was using some of the Hell's Angels as security men, saw events in the catering area differently:

We had got a company of caterers who were putting on burger bars and shops; they'd paid concessions to the Round Table for their space. I got called up on the walkie-talkie saying that they were being hassled by local gangsters who were asking for protection money and so I got in my jeep and went down there with the Hell's Angels, and the Hell's Angels found these guys, there were four or five of them, and escorted them off the site – there was no problem at all.

**Colin King, festival show director**

There are many different stories as to what started the fighting involving the Hell's Angels – I think one of the most reasonable ones was that a can of Coca-Cola was taken by one of the Hell's Angels from a stall that was being looked after by one of the local boys. That kicked off the trouble and later

**Hell's Angels flee from the caterers' security.** (Mike Sams)

World War Three would erupt – and that certainly affected my medical centre.

**Dr Dick Farrow, Clacton GP and Clacton Round Table**

The drinking and unruly behaviour continued throughout the morning, as the self-appointed custodians of law and order, the Hell's Angels, took vehicles belonging to caterers and the organisers for joyrides and rode their bikes purposely into the peaceful crowds:

There were two Austin Champs, I don't know where they'd come from – we had two blokes riding around checking on fires, then a bunch of Angels

ambushed them, pushed them out and took over. As they drove past another four or five got on, so there were now seven Angels in the truck, all shouting and driving around.

**Nigel Davers, Clacton Round Table**

I did witness the Hell's Angels driving around the site in the caterers' jeeps at one stage. We had a tent behind the stage with quite a few barrels of beer in there for our own consumption; it was to have been a meeting place for ourselves but we were so busy that we never got around to meeting there.

The Hell's Angels found it and I think they got well tanked-up and then things developed from there. I do understand that there may have been

**The Angels' bikes are attacked.** (Mike Sams)

a vendetta between the caterers and the Hell's Angels; there'd been trouble at other festivals.
**Graham Syrett, Clacton Round Table**

Whatever the truth of the matter, in the course of this fracas, property to the value of £6,000 belonging to Fine Caterers Ltd of Battersea was damaged, according to police records.

Meanwhile the music continued, with performances throughout Saturday morning from a number of lesser-known bands, but as noon approached the first of the major names of the time, Mungo Jerry, took to the stage. Lead singer, Ray Dorset, did his best to involve the crowd, which he did with some success, helped as the sun broke through the clouds and a party atmosphere evolved:

> Our office had a red double-decker bus sent down there, we were using it as a changing room and there was a bar on there and a DJ booth. I remember we were shooting a promo film for our forthcoming single; 'You Don't Have To Be In The Army To Fight In The War', so I think we were more occupied in looking at this big red bus and all the journalists that were on there; we were looking for promotion from them.
>
> John Godfrey, our bass player, had travelled down from London actually on the bus, and I think he'd had quite a few drinks on the way down to Weeley.
>
> Everybody was pretty merry by the time we actually got on the stage.
> **Ray Dorset, Mungo Jerry**

Despite having broken down on route and having had to be towed on to the site, the red double-decker bus became a landmark and the place to be for many of those backstage, artists and journalists alike. Those operating the bus, or at least the bar on board, were obviously doing a good job:

A fallen Angel.
(Mike Sams)

Guests were entertained in the double-decker in a manner above and beyond the call of duty.
*New Musical Express*, 4 September 1971

There was a big old London double-decker bus parked up behind the stage. It was a mobile bar, it was a sort of focal point. Although it didn't move anywhere, everybody was in there, all the bands … You couldn't get an alcoholic drink anywhere else on the festival site, it's no wonder it was so popular.
**Hoss Selfe, Weeley resident**

Despite regular announcements from the stage warning of the huge fire risk, further outbreaks occurred. Late Saturday morning saw the most dangerous incident of the entire festival, with fire spreading through a large area of the tinder-dry

**The Angels examine the damage.** (Mike Sams)

**Saturday midday with Mungo Jerry.** *(Clacton and Frinton Gazette)*

**Ray Dorset of Mungo Jerry.** (Mike Sams)

farmland. It engulfed all before it at an alarming rate, tents, vehicles and even part of the festival village that was in its way.

When the main event got going, fire became a huge fear, at the time I had a Triumph Herald convertible, and during the festival there was quite a major fire which took out a Triumph Herald, not mine fortunately, and another couple of vehicles and a motorbike and I looked at that and I thought 'wow!'

It was very frightening, the way the fire picked up and it just went. I remember in particular, we had what we called 'the village' with, maybe fifty large marquee tents, and the fire got within a few yards before we managed to put it out – my fear was that a fire would have gone through there like a hurricane, 'whoosh'

**Graham Syrett, Clacton Round Table**

One of the hats I wore was responsibility for our fire service. When the fires started someone came to me and told me to make a fire block to prevent the fire spreading. I asked how do you do that and he said, 'you just light a strip along the edge of the corn and that'll halt anything from that direction and protect the tents'.

So I did this, lit the fire and immediately the wind changed and the whole of the side of the field caught fire, then the hedge caught fire and then two telegraph poles. The fire brigade arrived and put the fire out in about three minutes, and then the firemen, who wanted to see the festival, said they'd better stay there for a while to check things over, and they had the time of their lives.

In another incident a car did catch fire. The petrol tank went up and was blown off the car and underneath an articulated truck that had about 50 gallons of fuel in. Another Round Table member, Roy Link, and I grabbed four of the old-fashioned fire extinguishers that you punch the top of to use, and we ran through this fire with blankets over our heads, stopped, put the extinguishers down to use them … and they were all duff, so we looked at each other with the fire completely surrounding us now, ran back and grabbed another four extinguishers and luckily we managed to put the fire out.

We had fifty of these extinguishers and after the festival only about ten had worked.
**Nigel Davers, Clacton Round Table**

We'd slept with our sleeping bags in the arena, and next day we returned to our tent to, well, check if it was still there. There were rumours of some trouble overnight, and the cornfield we had left was just burned stubble, there had been a fire. An American girl in a very thin hippy dress was wandering around in tears. She had lost her tent, passport, tickets home and all her money in the fire. My friend gave her a couple of quid.
**Tim Hillyar, festival fan**

One group of straw bivouacs and two cars were completely destroyed, a spark from a cooking fire started the blaze and dozens of hippy communes were destroyed in less than a minute. Some people managed to salvage just a guitar or a camera.
*Reporter:* What have you lost?'
*Tearful female: Oh, bloody everything*
**BBC Radio Report**

There had been an uneasy truce surrounding the Hell's Angels and the concessionaires, following the earlier fracas in the catering area of 'the village'. Some of the Angels were still taking their security role seriously – perhaps too seriously for many. At around 1 p.m. a call went out from the stage from an Angel called Joe, from the Cotswold Chapter, to fellow Angels, telling them that they were needed for firefighting duties. Shortly afterwards, a number of Angels were seen driving around in a Jeep. There

were at least four such vehicles on-site: one being used by festival organiser Colin King, and at least three belonging to caterers. At around this time, the chief constable and three other senior officers stopped a vehicle carrying nine Hell's Angels with sticks. They claimed to be security guards, and that they were driving the vehicle with permission, a claim that was later refuted by Colin King. Soon afterwards, these nine Angels were stopped again and were arrested for possessing offensive weapons and using threatening behaviour.

Around half an hour later, another disturbance involving Hell's Angels took place in the medical tent:

I remember one of the first casualties coming in was one of the local guys. His arm was hanging limply and he'd obviously had a very severe fracture of his upper arm. As I started treating him, I was then told that some of the Hell's Angels were coming in to the health centre because they thought I was shielding 'some of the enemy' and, looking back, I feel somewhat embarrassed by the fact that I started to spout the Geneva Convention - which they didn't really understand – but there were no problems in that respect.
**Dr Dick Farrow, Clacton GP and Clacton Round Table**

Dick Farrow and some other doctors were in the medical tent; it had a huge reception area and was then screened off for the doctors and the nurses and in the treatment area. Word had gone out to the Hell's Angels that one of their number was being treated in the medical tent and he was being held until the police could come and arrest him, so they were going to get together and smash up the medical tent and collect their man.

Another of the Round Table, a big man and a friend of mine, Tiny Singleton, was also helping. He came running in to tell me this and said, 'Talk with them while I go and get help. I'll try and get the police, but don't let them in whatever you do. Talk with them and just get them to calm down.'

Well, as he went out one side of the tent, this massive Hell's Angel came running in through the other tent, and I thought, he's not going to talk with anyone, he's running at full pelt and he's running towards the doctors. The only thing, besides myself, in there was the old-fashioned stretchers with the two poles and a canvas in-between, so I picked up this wooden pole, and it was fortunate that I'd trained in the Buddhist art of staff-fighting

… but I didn't know a lot about it. So I picked up this stretcher and I used this to try to stop the guy, by pushing the staff into his chest with the idea of winding him. But as I pushed it towards his chest and he ran forward he pushed it out the way, the pole flew out sideways and smacked him on the side of his head, knocking him out and gave him a 4 or 5in gash on the side of his head.

I then had screaming hysterics, thinking I'd killed him, so I got down on the ground and managed to wake him up, I said, 'Don't move, I'll get you a medic straight away and we'll get you stitched up.'

**A Hell's Angel examines his damaged bike.** (Mike Sams)

There was blood pouring out of the wound, which he touched and said, 'Are you stupid? If you stitch this up there'll be no scar; this'll be a battle scar.' He got up, pushed me out of the way and said, 'I don't want any stitching or anything. I want a scar that I can see.'

I then explained that no doctor was holding any Hell's Angel, so go and tell your mates, and with this he stumbled outside. There must have been twenty of them outside and they would have caused a lot of trouble.

**Nigel Davers, Clacton Round Table**

Following the mid-morning incident in the catering area, when the Hell's Angels had stormed Fine Caterers, a call had gone out from the concession-aires for assistance; they had decided to arrange their own security. By 3 p.m. these reinforcements had arrived on-site, and they were certainly capable of looking after the interests of the caterers.

The 'security men', also referred to by some as the 'pie-men', numbered forty or so, and included local 'heavies' and a number of tough-looking guys who had travelled to Weeley from London, cornered the Hell's Angels behind the stage area and viciously attacked them with iron bars, spades and pickaxe handles. The Hell's Angels also had an arsenal of weapons, including knives, iron bars and knuckledusters, but, despite these and their tough reputation, they were no match for the new arrivals, who had come prepared to settle scores.

Several of the Angels attempted to scale the 6ft-high wooden security fence surrounding the backstage area in an effort to escape the beating that was threatened, but those who remained or who were unable to escape suffered at the hands of these heavily armed and menacing guys.

The caterers then organised some lads to come down from London who went in behind the stage, smashed the bikes up and although the Angels looked rough and tough I think a large number of Angels went into the medical tent, but I think only one caterer went in – so they weren't that rough and tough.

**Graham Syrett, Clacton Round Table**

Police reinforcements had been built up during the day, but there was no police presence behind the stage, although they were stationed nearby, and by the time they arrived it was a bloody scene. Hell's Angels were dazed and injured, and in some cases their girlfriends were screaming hysterically. Worst still, many of their prized motorcycles had been attacked with sledgehammers and axes, and irreparably damaged, petrol tanks punctured and bodywork mangled.

A number of Hell's Angels were in need of medical treatment, in a few cases for very severe injuries. Dr Dick Farrow was on duty in the medical tent and was responsible for treating most of them:

We had a number, maybe fourteen or fifteen, of moderate to severe trauma cases, admitted in a relatively short period of time, I think it was between fifteen and thirty minutes. Ten arrived with head injuries and, apart from two fractured skulls and two fractured limbs, which were sent to Colchester, we dealt with the rest on-site.

I was told that there was a severely injured Hells Angel who'd been brought in, so I went outside … and I saw four Hell's Angels carrying a door, which I think had been commandeered, probably from the church, with an unconscious Hell's Angel lying on it. They put it down on the ground, and I knelt down and opened his eyelid, as I normally would, to see the state of the pupil, and I was somewhat surprised to see there was no eye there. Obviously that surprise was noticed by one of the chaps carrying this door, who said,

'Oh, don't worry about that, Doc. He lost that in Brighton last year.'

Some good work was done in a short time. In fact, on the Friday evening, because I was concerned about cover, I'd contacted the London Hospital, who sent down fifteen final-year medical students for a bit of job experience. They were extremely helpful and very supportive, and I think it's recorded that they put in over 164 stitches over a period of an hour and a half.

**Dr Dick Farrow, Clacton GP and Clacton Round Table**

Very few of the 'security men' remained in the backstage area after the violence, and so they were not apprehended. It's fair to assume that many of those who'd metered out the violence to the Angels had been able to blend in with the festival crowds and move on, avoiding any possible dealings with the police.

Surprisingly, most of the tens of thousands of music fans were unaware of the trouble that had kicked off behind the stage until they returned home and read about it in the national newspapers:

I knew nothing of the fights and troubles until I got home and my grand-mother was very concerned and asked me about the fighting, 'What fighting?', I asked... I'd seen none of it.

**Garry Bodenham, festival fan**

But for the small number of people on the festival site that had witnessed events, it had been a very frightening and potentially dangerous situation:

When the clash between the Hell's Angels and the caterers took place, the press were in the thick of it. It was like a war, but in this case they were faced by a load of caterers, really hard-nut caterers, partially local, partially from London who'd become fed up with the attitude and behaviour of these Hell's Angels ... then it exploded ... The caterers, they took iron bars, anything they could. They smashed their chopper motorcycles up, they smashed the Hell's Angels up and gave them 'what for'. It was a terrifying experience but the audience couldn't see it; the only people who saw it were the people behind the stage. There was blood everywhere. I can remember seeing Hell's Angels crying when they saw the damage to their bikes. I've never been so frightened in my life.

**Mike Sams, newspaper reporter**

The Angels were on-site and they were certainly a problem, and then they had a confrontation with some of the traders and their people. Quite a number of people ended up in the medical tent, but most of them were Hell's Angels, not the caterers. The police had a tent on-site, but they were basically not involved. They were kept in the tent and not called on to the site in any big way – until the trouble with the Hell's Angels, then they had to be called in. They took the Hell's Angels, and their motorcycles. The Hell's Angels might have looked the toughest, but they came off the worse.

**Graham Syrett, Clacton Round Table**

Despite the injuries that had been inflicted on the Hell's Angels, they refused to identify those responsible for the attack. They told police that their rules did not allow this and that they would settle things their own way. The implication was that more violence would follow, with the Angels suggesting more of their number would be summoned to even the score. They were told by the police that this would not be tolerated, and, amid scuffles and heated arguments, forty-one Hell's Angels were rounded up by a large squad of police officers, removed from the site and taken to Weeley Village Hall, which was doubling as the festival police station:

I was a sergeant with quite a few years behind me, so not the first time I'd come across a violent situation. I had a lot of young policemen with me, fresh from training school, at the time. It was a horrific experience for them, although I think later they enjoyed it – it was something to talk about in the pub afterwards.

I didn't see the actual violence on the Hell's Angels by the hired thugs, but minutes later I saw the aftermath of it, wondering what to do with all these bodies lying about, some of them were in a very bad way. There were a number of stretcher cases, though we didn't have stretchers.

I'd only been there five minutes and there was still violence going on. We had our Chief Constable and Deputy Chief Constable wading in with their fists. They were well past that sort of thing, but they enjoyed it. We did push them out of the way

**Police impound the Angels' bikes.** (Mike Sams)

and said 'you're too bloody old for this sort of thing.'
**Derrick Thomas, police officer**

Amid the turmoil and confusion, several arrests were made and a number of people held. Some police officers were involved in processing the prisoners ready for their transfer to various police stations in the area:

> The reputation of these Hell's Angels had gone before them. They were a dirty and dishevelled load of bikers ... the hard men of this world and based themselves on the American Hell's Angels. They were arrogant; they even thought they could take on the police. There were no nice people amongst them. We had very little conversation with them, except to tell them when we arrested

them. We locked them in Weeley Village Hall. It was just somewhere to put them before we carted them off. It was very hot in the hall and, after a while, they turned into very meek people, asking for food and drink and they became very polite about it.
**Derrick Thomas, police officer**

All the motorcycles were put on a trailer and taken to Police HQ, where they were put in a garage; there were twenty-five or thirty Hell's Angels' chopper bikes there. They were real Hell's Angels, and they hadn't washed, they absolutely stank. One guy had one fingerless glove on. He was told to take off his jacket, belt ...

'I can't take my glove off,' he said.

'Why can't you take your glove off?

**The Hells Angels and the jeeps.** (Mike Sams)

'This is the glove. When I was initiated into Hell's Angels this is the glove they gave me and I can't take it off.'

We kept their bikes for three or four weeks, but then arrangements were made for them all to come down en-masse to pick up their bikes.
**Brian Higgleton, Police officer**

We were told that the Hell's Angels were trying to take over the place. I, personally, had nothing to do with the arrests, but we were called in to escort them to Colchester following their arrests. We were in these mini buses, and one of the lads threw some of his sandwiches amongst them, and they were fighting each other for a slice of bread – they were a terrible sort of people, I'd never seen anything like it really, and when you saw others that made out that they were Hell's Angels, they were just like little boys compared to this lot. These were the real, real McCoy, you know, beards, scruffy … They wore several layers of clothes, and they urinated on their clothes. They'd have jeans on with a hole in them and they'd put on another pair on top of them. Some of them had three or four pairs of jeans on, all of them filthy dirty.

Sergeant Turner was at the back door of the old Queens Street Police Station in Colchester, where we took them, and before we came in with them, he'd been to the old Hippodrome cinema and borrowed one of their pump spray things that they used to clean the cinema out with and, as the Hell's Angels walked through the door, he was pump spraying them with this scented spray which, of course, they objected to because it was clean. I just fell over laughing, it was so funny to see and Sergeant Turner was saying 'Cor, Christ, get this lot clean.'

They hadn't got many cells at Colchester. I think some of them went on to Chelmsford … there must have been eighteen or twenty of these people. Their bikes were put on a trailer and chained down, and I remember, as they chained them down, the exhausts and all the metal was crunching, 'cos we had flat trailers behind Land Rovers, and these bikes were all taken up to Police HQ at Chelmsford … they were just dumped on the back, it was quite heart breaking really. I think if they could have seen what was happening to their bikes, because their bikes were their pride and joy, I think they might well have stood there crying. I believe there were two or three bikes that were never claimed, they stayed up at Chelmsford for some time, then I think they were sold.
**Brian Simpson, police officer**

A story our village policeman told me was about the Hell's Angels. He came over and said, 'You'll never believe it, those Hell's Angels had to be stripped and the leader of the pack, well he didn't want to be stripped, "I don't want anyone to see me" he said. He was crying, he was filthy dirty outside, but everything underneath, all his underwear was pure white spotless and he didn't want anyone to know that he'd bathed and had clean underwear!'
**Ena Wade, Weeley resident**

They weren't very nice people, they'd got away with blackmail at other festivals and they thought this was the life for them, but it didn't turn out that way – in fact, it stopped them turning out at other festivals. They learnt their lesson at Weeley. Several of them ended up with prison sentences, I'm glad it did; it seemed to stop violence at festivals.
**Derrick Thomas, police officer**

The national press were already fascinated by events at Weeley. Those in the press area were in the right place to witness the fracas that erupted. There were just so many newsworthy stories coming from the festival and, with what was seen by many journalists as 'an explosion of violence,' a front-page story about this tiny Essex village was guaranteed on every Sunday newspaper.

Not only were the national newspapers telling the story; the music and alternative press was fascinated by Weeley. A report from underground newspaper *FreeFrendz* summed up the Angels episode very well:

So the Angels arrive, stomp around and generally behave like some army of occupation. They take over stage security – complete with wooden clubs to underline the point as they check passes. Later they try and rip off the concessionaires and get trashed.

Fuzz [police] arrived to try to cool things.

A vigilante committee forms, consisting of security men (very heavies – out of work commandos etc.) and stage hands. Armed with monkey wrenches, clubs, sledge hammers etc., they march on the Angels who have moved to a small area back stage, because they are scared.

Fractured skull, many badly beaten up. Most of them wisely jumped over the wall the second they saw what was coming. Then the peace-loving vigilantes smashed up the Angels' beloved bikes.

Perhaps the Angels will learn from this tragedy that violence is not the answer. There's always someone tougher than you.

**FreeFrendz, 16 September 1971**

There were also television and radio reporters on-site. One journalist witnessed the start of the violence between the caterers, their security team and the Hell's Angels:

It's hard to estimate how many pop fans made the pilgrimage to Weeley in Essex this weekend, when the festival was originally granted a licence it was for just 10,000 – some say 150,000 are there now. With numbers like that, it's perhaps not surprising that violence flared, certainly it's the first pop festival where there've been more arrests under the Public Order Act, than there have for drug offences.

When the violence started our reporter was there:

When I arrived at Weeley it was hot and dusty with 80,000 people squashed into the arena – 'Everything's going fine,' the organiser said, but I'd heard there'd been some trouble from a band of Hell's Angels, so I went to a tent behind the stage to talk to them …

*'In a brotherhood you can call on any bloke who's in the brotherhood in any part of the country and he'll help you, he'll put you up, he'll feed you, he'll keep you, he'll clothe you.'*

'Is Hell's Angels a brotherhood then?'

*'It's a brotherhood man, we're brothers all through and through, Angels is a way of life, and everybody backs everybody else …'*

[Fight starts]

*'What's happening, what's up, who are we scrapping?'*

While we were talking some Angels rushed into the tent and started to pick up chairs and tables. I made a quick rush to the door to be met by a gang of non-Angels armed with sledge hammers, shovels and iron bars. They started to smash up the bikes, and when later I went back into the tent a number of Angels were laying on the floor in need of hospital treatment.

Who was responsible and why?

Caterer: *'The Hell's Angels came over to Fine caterers and smashed it to smithereens, smashed up our ovens the whole bit – and when we ask the police to get them off the site they say they won't take them off – so we've had to put 'em off ourselves'*

Almost mob rule in a situation of charge and counter-charge, certainly the police moved in after that.

For Major General F.J. Piggot of the Parish Council's festival committee, this was systematic of all that he'd feared:

'*My gloomy prognostications have been fulfilled ... I told them that they were handling something about which none of us really knew what we were talking about.*'

You're saying now that you think it's become uncontrollable?

'*I won't say uncontrollable, because I have the utmost confidence in the police, but it's getting pretty near that as far as I can see*'

But Viv Speck, whose brainchild the festival is ... sees the violence as a minority incident, not affecting the vast majority of pop fans and disagrees with the General:

'*This is a lot of nonsense, because if you'd like to go down to the police station and talk to Mr Duke [assistant chief constable] with his estimates, we've got 150,000 people here, taking out this element of Hell's Angels, which he abhors anyway, we haven't had any arrests ... and I'm sure he'd say to you, what he said to me, that this element has got to be crushed ... and  Mr Duke came in*

**A stretcher case for the medical tent.** (PA Photos/ TopPhoto)

*here and cleared these people off, and we've had no other problems'*

Certainly while I was there, apart from some bad trips, a couple of drug arrests and thefts from tents there were no other problems ... and certainly, no more violence and no more Angels.

Major General Piggot, however, is still dubious:

*'If you're going to get a hundred thousand people together in one place then almost certainly they're likely to have violence of one sort or another, and therefore, whether it is in the public interest to allow these enormous gatherings to take place seems to me to be very doubtful'.*

But Vic Speck has no doubts. Does he see the festival as a success?

*'Absolutely, look in the arena, it's full, it's got 80,000 people in it, and I go up on stage there and they all know me as Vic, and we get a jolly good cheer ... it's great'*

Would you do all this again?

*'Oh yes, I think so ... Yes'*

**Radio news report.**

With the removal of the Hell's Angels and with the police restoring law and order, calm once again returned to the entire festival site. However, information was received by police that more groups of Hell's Angels were on their way to the festival. The chief constable decided that it was undesirable for any number of Hell's Angels to be on the site, so police crews on the road stopped a number of groups of motorcyclists and persuaded them not to continue their journey.

More than 200 police statements were taken, many giving the Hell's Angels' versions of events that took place on that Saturday afternoon:

After I parked my motorbike I went to the beer tent. Sometime during the afternoon I was sitting having a beer, when about five blokes set about me for no reason. I don't remember what happened, but I had cuts on my head. I couldn't recognise anyone who was there but I do remember a big dog being there, which, I think, belonged to one of the blokes that attacked me.

We were employed by the organisers to keep people off the stage. Most of the time we stayed near the beer tent. During the early part of the afternoon I was in a jeep on the site with about 10 Hell's Angels. The jeep stalled and a gang of blokes attacked us with shovels and iron bars. We all jumped out of the jeep. I fell face down on the ground and someone hit me a number of times on the head with a shovel. I saw one bloke in the group. He was short, fair hair receding at the front, a small beard. He seemed to be the leader.

I walked round looking for the others. As I was walking towards them someone hit me on the head from behind with an iron bar. As I fell to the ground I saw a big bloke with a blue shirt run past me. I heard someone shout, 'there's one'. So I got up and ran. I saw one of my mates, he took me to the First Aid Tent.

Whilst walking around the site we picked up whatever sticks we could find and when we reached the medical tent there was about 50 Angels. There we met a group of police who stopped us and tried to quiet everyone down, this took about an hour. Injured people were being brought to the tent and a group of the men who attacked us went by. Eventually the police let us go back to the beer tent to see what damage had been done to our bikes. When we were climbing over the fence to escape we heard the bikes being smashed up but I could not see anything.

My bike, a BSA, had a half inch diameter hole in the bottom of the oil tank which appeared to have been done by a pick axe, and a smashed headlight.

I don't know of any reasons for the violence to take place.

**Extracts from police statements made by Hell's Angels**

Police also took statements from others who witnessed the violence:

I have a stall selling food stuffs at Weeley Pop Festival and I have been conducting business since Wednesday 25th August on the Festival grounds. This morning at around 11am about twenty Hell's Angels took over two of the vehicles and were riding around the grounds in them. Myself, and some of my colleagues, got the vehicles back from them. About 30 minutes later, Number 2 Champ [another 'jeep' style vehicle] which is an unregistered vehicle, was taken by seven Hell's Angels from near one of my stalls near the medical tent. They drove it away and had it for a while, as I and my colleagues were looking for them. We eventually found the vehicle near to the campsite. We took the vehicle back into our possession and drove away leaving the Hell's Angels there. After about fifty yards we ran out of petrol, so we had to leave it whilst we went for petrol. As I returned I saw a large number of Hell's Angels, possibly around sixty, milling around the vehicle causing damage.

**Extract from police statement made by a concessionaire**

Although a large police presence had been called upon to deal with the violence, once the Hell's Angels were moved on, some officers were able to enjoy a relaxing time, behind the stage area:

After the police had been called in to deal with the Hell's Angels trouble, some of them remained behind the stage and, like the Angels, they also found our beer tent. Not only had the Angels been tucking in quite nicely, but later some members of the police force were also enjoying the beer. There were also a lot of young ladies associated with some of the bands. Some police officers were enjoying the festival more than others.

A couple of us went in, with my pick-up truck, to take the beer out; there were about ten casks and just two were left untouched. The police were not happy. Their language and body language suggested they were not pleased.

**Graham Syrett, Clacton Round Table**

Festival director Colin King has always held a different view from most others present about who caused the trouble at the festival. Earlier on the Saturday, the Hell's Angels working with him on security had 'removed' a small group of 'local gangsters', who, it was believed, were demanding protection money from the caterers. He played down the incident, claiming it was all 'blown up by the press':

There was a big panic call from these guys saying 'they've come back, they've come back,' and they came back with forty other people – their 'friends' – and just laid into the Hell's Angels bikes … attacked them and damaged the bikes and beat up the Hell's Angels in revenge for being kicked off the site. I don't think there were many arrests, if any at all. It was all blown up by the press. In any city of 150,000 you're going to get punch-ups on a Saturday night, and that's really what it was.

**Colin King, festival show director**

# IT'S ALL HAPPENING

By Saturday afternoon, the organisation of the event, such as it was, had started to struggle in a number of areas. Round Table members and volunteers had been working for long periods without rest or breaks, the gates were left and entry to the Weeley Festival was now open to everyone without charge.

The arena was already packed to capacity, with an estimated crowd of up to 150,000 on-site, and concerns were expressed by the assistant police constable and by the chief fire officer about the lack of emergency exits. They both warned Vic Speck that the limited number of 'gateways' would be totally inadequate if an emergency evacuation were to be necessary, and asked for a large part of the security fence to be taken down before dusk.

The weather was hot and sunny – great for the festival-goers, but a cause for concern in the medical tent:

> One of the problems with Weeley was that it was an extremely hot weekend, and this in itself created problems. In those days people were not so conscious of sunburn for example, so we had cases of sunburn and several cases of dehydration, because a lot of the young people were in the arena for many, many hours at a time and they were not getting out to rehydrate themselves, and that led to other medical problems.

We were getting very concerned late Saturday afternoon, that the fans just weren't looking after themselves in the sun, so I went up on to the side of the stage to ask Colin King, who was running the whole shoot, to tell the crowd to drink plenty of water and go to the toilet when necessary and to watch their skin. To my amazement, he went on to the stage and announced to the thousands out there that they were going to have to listen very carefully because he was going to introduce Dr Dick, who was doing a great job, and suddenly I was thrust out to speak to many thousands of youngsters … certainly the largest audience of my life.

I actually got a cheer, I have to say – with all modesty!

**Dr Dick Farrow, Clacton GP and Clacton Round Table**

The medical tent was kept busy throughout the festival, all manner of emergencies and more mundane medical problems were dealt with over the weekend by Dr Farrow:

> I was told that some girl had what started as a stomach complaint; by the time I got to her, I thought she was having a baby. I believe it was Dick Farrow who said, 'Take me to her.' so he's carrying his bag and I'm walking in front and this is right in the pop area with thousands of people

sitting down and we're stepping around people sitting down. I accidently put my foot straight through a classical guitar that a guy had. I straight away said, 'Don't worry, we'll pay for it, come and see me afterwards.'

We got to the girl, she wasn't having a baby, she just had stomach cramps.

So I went back to the tent and this guy came along and said, 'You put your foot through my classical guitar.'

I said, 'Yep, very sorry ... how much?'

He replied, 'It cost me £45,' which was a lot of money in those days, but I said, 'OK ... it's a shame we've got to pay out, so less money will be going to charity.'

So he said. 'Well who's making all the money out of this?'

'Nobody,' I said. 'It's Round Table who've organised it and every single penny is going to charity, and not only aren't we making anything out of it, but I'm about £50 out of pocket myself, just by helping.'

He looked at me and said 'Well, if you're not making anything then forget it, shake hands and forget it.' He shook my hand and walked off saying, 'I hope you make a lot of money,' and that was the sort of people we saw again and again and again.
**Nigel Davers, Clacton Round Table**

Not only were proper medical records kept of all the patients that were treated over the weekend, but Dick Farrow had the foresight to make copious notes, in case another festival ever took place at Weeley:

One of the things I was determined to do – because there had been no previous records to help me know what to expect – was to try and collate some statistics from the pop festival, and three of my secretaries did a rota for the seventy-two hours from the Friday morning to the Monday morning and registered every patient that came into the health centre. There were 1,700 in that seventy-two hours and, as you can imagine, their needs covered everything that an ordinary accident and emergency department at a major hospital would cover.
**Dr Dick Farrow, Clacton GP and Clacton Round Table**

And still the music continued. There had been concern within Weeley village that sleep would be impossible. But with the wind strength and direction in their favour, and the sound system being relatively primitive compared to the equipment available today, most people living close to the festival site were not troubled by the music from the stage:

I did go around one evening and, I could hear it louder at my home, with the wind blowing, than you could in front of the stage. Those towards Thorpe-le-Soken got the best of everything – they could hear the whole lot, sitting in their gardens!

My Dad went over there, and dad being dad, he just took it in his stride. I think he was a little bit overwhelmed at the amount of people; I don't think he'd had any idea that there were going to be that many people on his fields! But he was the sort of person who liked to talk and natter and look and think. I think he was quite impressed in some ways ... depressed in others maybe! Especially after people had gone and the mess was to be cleared up.
**David Weeley, Weeley resident, son of Roger Weeley, landowner**

I heard a great deal of the music, although I can't say that I saw much of it on stage. I have to say, on the Saturday night, having been up there on-site for two or three days non-stop I was greeted by my wife who said, 'I think I'm going to take you home for some sleep' and we drove home. Now,

I live by Clacton seafront, and it was amazing that the music seemed clearer in my front porch than it was actually up on-site.

**Dr Dick Farrow, Clacton GP and Clacton Round Table**

## Was Wally Really There?

One of the legends of music events throughout the seventies was a crowd chant for 'Wally'. The origins of this chant are lost in 'the mists of time', but various versions of the story abound.

There are those who believe it originated from a stage announcement for Wally to meet his friends, with the crowd taking up the call. Or perhaps it was innocently started by someone eager to meet up with Wally and desperately calling the name, as he searched in vain for his friend? The most frequently heard version is that the chant was first heard at the Isle of Wight festival in 1970; nonetheless, some firmly maintain that it was first heard in the fields of Hall Farm, Weeley.

Wally's true origins and history will probably never be known, but is it just coincidence that 'Where's Wally' books rely on the reader searching for a 'lost Wally' in a large crowd?

Whatever Wally's history there were many calling for him at Weeley:

The arena was full of recumbent horizontal bodies on Saturday afternoon, when somebody started the now famous 'Where's Wally' chant. Apparently a hit at the Isle of Wight festival the year before where someone was genuinely looking for their friend Wally, this also did the rounds at Weeley. We were amused. I often wonder if the children's book 'Where's Wally', where you have to find a little guy in a striped top among hundreds of others, originated from that call.

**Tim Hillyar, festival fan**

I do wonder if the Wally chant started at Weeley. In my mind it did. I was sitting at the top left-hand corner, quite near the stage, and there were loads of people up on a … well, it was a big wall or fence that they'd constructed to keep people out of the arena so that they would supposedly go through the main entrance and show their tickets. Loads of people were up on this thing and … they were all chanting, 'Where's Wally'… I don't think Wally ever existed, but it continued and by the Sunday the whole place, the whole festival, everyone, was on a desperate search for Wally – I didn't find him, but I did join in.

**Tony O'Neil, festival fan**

Yes, the Wally thing certainly seemed to come from Weeley. I remember a guy wandering through the audience calling for him as if he was a lost friend, and the rest of us took up the call. One thing I can't be sure of is whether that was the birth of the legend! As you probably remember, it was a common call at festivals and gigs for years after.

**Garry Bodenham, festival fan**

# LISTEN TO THE MUSIC

During the afternoon and early evening, the music continued from the Weeley stage. Fairfield Parlour and Stone the Crows, featuring Maggie Bell, had followed the lunchtime performance by Mungo Jerry. But of all the artists that were to appear on the Saturday, one performance was anticipated more than any other.

Barclay James Harvest were a popular progressive British rock band, famed for albums featuring orchestral arrangements of their songs, and it was with an orchestra that they were due to perform at Weeley, something that had never been attempted before at an open-air pop festival. The logistics of setting up a forty-piece orchestra in a cornfield were certainly challenging.

Despite the festival's music organiser, Colin King's intention of having a seamless programme with no gaps – 'as one band leaves the stage the next will appear straight away' – the wait for Barclay James Harvest, already delayed by several hours, was considerable. They were expected on stage at 5 p.m., but it was nearly 9 p.m. before their performance started. Sections of the crowd were starting to show their impatience, but the performance they eventually gave was considered to be one of the highlights of the entire Weeley weekend:

We kind of stole the event I think. When we talk about Weeley, people's memories always seem to gravitate to when we were on. I think the timing was perfect. The sun was going down and the stage lighting started to have some effect, and we just went on and filled the air with melodic sounds.
**Woolly Wolstenholme, Barclay James Harvest**

Martyn Ford had the responsibility of putting the orchestra together and conducting the performance. Although at the time he was a relative newcomer, he has since gone on to work with some of the top names in rock music and been involved with many of the best albums ever recorded:

I had just started conducting and arranging around this time and I had formed my own orchestra, made up of musicians hand-picked from four music colleges. Unlike the established orchestras, which were made up of older musicians who didn't really like pop music, I was putting together orchestras where the musicians were all aged just 18 to 22 and wanted to be there.

Barclay James Harvest management said, 'Can we have an orchestra for a festival appearance at Weeley, near Clacton?' I called around and got forty or so musicians together and said 'meet outside the Royal Academy of Music,' and we travelled down there by coach.

I remember it was very hot. The audience were getting restless waiting for the band and it took an hour or more to set up. We had to arrange all the seating on the stage. The band set up on stage behind the orchestra. They were on some sort of dais and I was conducting the band and the orchestra, though I don't think the band were taking any notice of me. We needed something like thirty or forty microphones. There was no chance

of a soundcheck beforehand and I think the first couple of songs might have sounded a bit shaky, but it soon came right and it was hugely successful.

I remember it was late in the day and the sun was going down … there was an amazing atmosphere.
**Martyn Ford, composer and conductor**

**Mungo Jerry with a security dog for support.**
(Getty Images)

The best performance of them all as far as I was concerned – and its only my personal choice – was Barclay James Harvest, particularly because we did something that had never been done before: we put on a forty-piece orchestra in the middle of a field in the middle of nowhere, together with a rock band, and although that had happened before inside halls at concerts, it had never happened out in the open. Jim Marshall, who was the guy that had to mix all the sound, he was very excited about the prospect. It took a long time to put it together on stage, but when they eventually came to put it together ... everyone just stopped in their tracks and you could see people's jaws drop open, because they'd never heard a sound like this in the middle of a field. It was extraordinary and that for me was one of the highlights.
**Colin King, festival show director**

Barclay James Harvest, 'Mockingbird': I remember seeing them performing that, it was wonderful, and I remember seeing a huge lighting screen either side of the stage, which was projecting liquid wheel effects, sort of hallucinogenic 1970s effects, and I'd never seen anything like that before.
**Tony O'Neil, festival fan**

**Singer Maggie Bell and guitarist Les Harvey of Scottish blues band Stone the Crows.** (Getty Images)

**Stone the Crows on stage.**
(Clacton and Frinton Gazette)

I remember Barclay James Harvest giving a tremendous show with 'Mockingbird'. They'd come with a sizeable orchestra, but it took well over an hour and a half for them to set up. Everybody was getting very edgy about this, but when they started playing it was just ecstasy all around; it really was a tremendous performance from them and really enjoyable.

**Mike Sams, newspaper reporter**

One set that really sticks in my mind was Barclay James Harvest, who played with an orchestra. It took ages to set up, but the sound was superb in the early evening air and they used a mellotron, I have been a fan ever since. I still play 'Mockingbird' to this day.
**Tim Hillyar, festival fan**

I remember 'Mockingbird' being played by Barclay James Harvest and that just wafted over the whole of Weeley. It was a lasting memory, and that was just fantastic.
**Tony Haggis, festival fan**

Although a very eventful Saturday was coming to an end, the music from the stage continued, with many thousands of fans choosing to stay in the arena rather than returning to the campsite. With the continuing delays, a number of big name performers were forced to perform in the middle of the night. Al Stewart followed Barclay James Harvest, after they'd 'bowed off to tumultuous applause' (*New Musical Express*), and it was around midnight before King Crimson played their set. Curved Air had waited so long that they gave up and went home without performing, and those wanting to see the Groundhogs waited until the early hours. It was after 2 a.m. when festival regular Rory Gallagher got to the stage. Despite the late – or early – hour, he gave an energetic and enthusiastic performance. Mott the Hoople was, at the time, an up-and-coming band. It was daylight before they got to perform. 'We've been up all night waiting to play – we're tired. We're not complaining, but the music could be better,' said band member Ian Hunter.

Everyone had their favourites:

King Crimson were there. They were my hero band, wonderful; they came on late very, two or three hours after they'd been billed. And I was still awake for Rory Gallagher. He gave a wonderful show. I remember he was on very, very late at night.
**Tony O'Neil, festival fan**

I just wanted to get to there to make some sounds. I loved the Groundhogs, they were my favourite band then, and I was really excited about seeing the Pink Fairies; they played and made my day. I remember enjoying myself so much and being really excited. I saw Rory Gallagher but I missed King Crimson. I slept through their set.
**Garry Bodenham, festival fan**

I vaguely remember King Crimson before falling asleep. I thought the best set of the weekend was from the Groundhogs. I think they were on around 3 a.m. I bought their album, *Thank Christ for the Bomb*, on the strength of that set. They were awesome. My friend woke me up for Mott the Hoople.
**Tim Hillyar, festival fan**

We were lucky enough to talk to many of the stars. My own personal favourite was Rory Gallagher. He didn't start playing till 2 a.m., and he played until 4 a.m. He was absolutely worn out and wanted somewhere to sleep, so he slept in our tent. It was an old scouting tent and quite large. It was that sort of atmosphere; people would offer a tent, offer their hospitality to the stars – all the bands were very tired – and you felt like a star yourself.

Because I was reporting on the event I had to chance to meet nearly all of the bands. The trouble was the groups were lined up in such numbers, playing back-to-back ... that they were very tired, and certainly I was very tired. And sadly, I didn't get to see some of them that I wanted to. The group members that I spoke to thought it was great and a real experience. None of them had heard of Weeley, but still came. They just wanted somewhere to show off their musical talent, and Weeley gave them that opportunity.

**Mike Sams, newspaper reporter**

After all the troubles of the previous afternoon with the fights and arrests, calm had descended on the festival site by Saturday evening. Despite the huge number of people, all in the close confines of just three fields and with few facilities, the atmosphere was one of reconciliation and harmony. Many of the music fans chose to remain in the arena, either relaxing in their sleeping bags, or just spending a night underneath the stars. The official police report made the point that love and peace ruled:

From dusk on Saturday onwards, there was virtually no disorder. Music was provided throughout Saturday night, and, although the licence expired at 6 a.m. on Sunday morning, was still provided live by groups or from recordings until 6 a.m. on Monday.

**Official police report**

The majority of those at the festival were flower power hippy types, with long hair – 'Hi Man, peace'. They didn't cause any trouble. You've never seen crowds like it; they came from everywhere. Everyone was very happy, very content. There were no footpaths; you had to step over all these people – some naked, some having sex, some sleeping. It was very difficult stepping over thousands of people.

**Peter Whent, police officer**

Those away from the festival woke up to the Sunday newspapers with headlines screaming about violence and stories of thousands of festival-goers running scared:

**Hell's Angels In Pop Festival Terror**

**60 Held After 'Angels' Battles At Pop Festival**

**Angels In Fight At Festival**

**60 Arrested In Pop Battle**

But by Monday morning they were talking of an outbreak of gentleness amongst the thousands of youngsters, who'd just gone to Weeley for a fun weekend and to enjoy the music.

The 'Jesus Tent', originally suggested by the Bishop of Colchester, was manned throughout by the Colchester Council of Churches and the Salvation Army. The church of St Andrew, the tiny Weeley parish church was right in the centre of the festival site, and many locals feared for its security prior to the event, but it remained open throughout the festival and was respected by the festival crowds:

The church was right in the middle of all this. It's a beautiful little church and it wasn't abused; there was no graffiti. They all respected it. And there were the Hare Krishna people here as well, ringing their bells and calming people.

**Ena Wade, Weeley resident**

During the weekend the united churches provided more than 900 gallons of tea, soup and coffee, as well as supplying pies, cakes and bread to hungry music fans. A team from London arrived on Saturday evening to assist the Clacton Salvation Army; they came with blankets and clothing, which were passed on to 200 people within minutes of their arrival. A collection was ongoing, organised by Shelter, the charity for the homeless, for those who had lost tents and belongings in the earlier fires at

**It is Mott the Hoople's turn to take to the stage.** (Getty Images)

the festival. Coca-Cola tins were passed around and festival-goers were invited to donate 1p or 2p pieces. A total of £653 was collected overall. A Shelter spokesman was overwhelmed by the response: 'From a charity point of view, I have never seen anything like it. Young people are really identifying with the charities.'

**Hare Krishnas were everywhere at the time.**
(Mike Sams)

Although I didn't see him, I remember reports of disc jockey John Peel working in the Release tent and helping at the soup kitchens.
**Mike Sams, newspaper reporter**

Food donations were made to the free food kitchen, many from festival-goers themselves, and according

to one newspaper the amenities were made good use of. The newspaper certainly made the food area sound more exotic than it really was:

Hundreds of penniless fans gathered round a free food kitchen where hippies from all over the world sat round the 'Glastonbury pot', centre of many wild hippy scenes.

A goulash stew, made from food given by other hippies boiled in an old dustbin.

Visitors to the site were greeted by hippie beggars collecting money to keep the free food kitchen going. 'We are providing an essential for hippies who are starving. It saves them from poaching and begging in the village, a scene we don't want,' one helper was reported as saying.

**Unidentified newspaper report**

By late Sunday morning, there was very little space to move within the arena. The star acts, Rod Stewart and The Faces and T.Rex, were due to appear later in the day, but one of the big successes of the festival took to the stage around lunchtime. Lindisfarne were just starting to receive popular acclaim, with songs like 'Fog on the Tyne' and 'We Can Swing Together'. The band had also become a favourite of the music press:

Somebody bangs their foot and away they go … I don't think it will be too long before they become an attraction of international repute.

*New Musical Express*, 4 September 1971

The first thing we asked was, 'Where's Weeley?' 'Cos it wasn't somewhere we were familiar with. We drove for hours to get there. Going up to Essex from London in those days could take a long time. The roads weren't that hot, although we were up and down the road to Harwich to get the boat to Europe a lot, so we knew the way, vaguely, but it seemed to take forever and then the traffic was so bad. But then when we got there we just got this feeling, with the huge number of people – you could feel it in the air.

I wasn't really aware of just how many people were there until it was our turn to go on stage, I mean, you could hear them, but you could always hear them, the cheering when you were backstage at a festival, you knew there were a lot of folks … but when it came time for us to go on, I remember climbing up … I think it was a ladder, I don't even know if they had steps at the back of the stage … and as my head became level with the stage and I could see, this crowd just seemed to go on forever. It was enormous, the biggest number of people I'd ever seen in my life, and I think I got, sort of, stage fright for a couple of seconds and stopped dead – and then received a hefty shove in the middle of my back from one of the management behind me. And the next thing I knew, we were playing, and that was it – off we went.

I think we all got a bit intoxicated by it. There were just so many people; we got such an amazing reaction. The band was just starting to happen, it was almost like … we didn't realise how popular we were until we got that number of people in one place at the same time.

**Ray Laidlaw, Lindisfarne**

The whole site was alive by the time Lindisfarne's set came to an end, and their encore of 'Clear White Light' went down a storm!

Julie Felix was a big star of the day, but having to follow Lindisfarne's superb performance couldn't have been easy for her. Dressed in a long black velvet kaftan, she at first struggled to get a response from the crowd, but after singing her best-known song, 'If I Could', the audience started to warm to her, and her genteel folk songs certainly calmed the mood of the crowd down:

It was a hot day in the summer, I wore a kind of hippy dress and I was five months pregnant, but it didn't show. The part I remember was when we were on stage and somebody was coming on after us and they were hammering in the drum kit, which was rather off-putting.

It was one of those festivals that happened before people really got into the commercial side of things, and that made it very spontaneous and special. I was at the height of my career at the time, so it was a real privilege to be part of the line-up.

The size of the audience was unbelievable, it was like being in another dimension, I'd played before at the Isle of Wight and I remember being completely in awe and it was the same thing at Weeley. There were multitudes of people and there was something almost unrealistic about it; it was magical.

I also remember receiving a cheque for charity, (Release) I was quite honoured that I was the one that was picked out to do that.

There was something very special and refreshing about those early festivals. Although Weeley was in 1971, it still had the feeling of the sixties. Anything was possible, anything could happen and you could just be yourself.
**Julie Felix, Performer**

I didn't have time to meet many of the stars, but I did meet Julie Felix … she only came up to my waist. I doubt she was even 5ft tall – a very tiny girl. As she stood on the stage she turned round and said, 'by the way – my fee, don't bother with it. Put it in the pot for charity', which I thought was fantastic.
**Nigel Davers, Clacton Round Table**

I remember Julie Felix, I thought she was fabulous, 'cos I'd never seen her before; she gave a really relaxed, really professional kind of performance.
**Robert Broughton, Edgar Broughton Band**

**Weeley's church register shows the baptisms of Lucy and Sharon, which took place during the festival.**

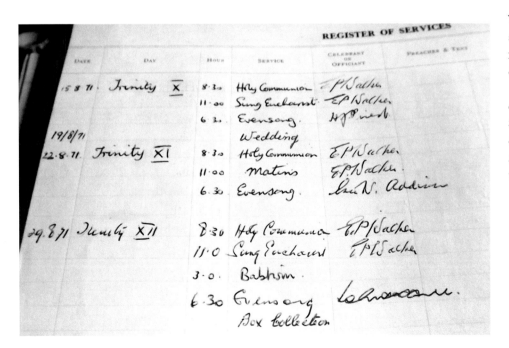

Whilst Julie Felix was entertaining the crowds on stage during that hot Sunday afternoon, two Weeley residents were making a star appearance of their own, just yards away from the stage.

Life went on in the village, despite the excitement of the festival. Of the four church services held in St Andrew's Church in the centre of the festival site on that day, the baptisms of little Lucy Ann Dear and Sharon Louise Wade were of great importance to their families.

My daughter Lucy was christened at Weeley church during the festival. We had people coming from Canada, one was a godfather, so it had to go ahead, and the baptism was booked long before we knew about the festival. We were a bit worried at first as to whether we could go ahead, but we were given special passes to drive down to the church and when you were in the church you just wouldn't

have known that there was anybody else outside, it was just like a normal day. Yet it was all going on around three sides of the church.
**Pam Dear, Weeley resident and Lucy's mother**

The congregation were in fine voice within the church as the acts continued with their performances on the stage.

The Grease Band were originally the backing band of Joe Cocker, and had appeared at the Woodstock festival with him fronting the band. But during 1970 the band had released albums in their own right. Speculation was rife that Cocker would reunite with the band at Weeley, recreating the Woodstock experience. Sadly he didn't, although the festival organiser, Colin King, claimed that he was at the festival. Cocker wasn't the only star that was on-site, according to King, but did not appear:

Although the performance by Barclay James Harvest was my high point of the festival, there was another amazing event that nobody else knows about, because it was only me that experienced it. What had happened was that The Grease Band had arrived, and there were rumours that Joe Cocker had arrived with them and that he was going to play, but that was unlikely. I was asked to go to the caravan dressing room backstage … there were two guys, long hair, beards, dark glasses strumming guitars, singing, 'I'll get by with a little help from my friends'. I thought, that's Joe Cocker … I looked at the other guy 'Oh my God', it was John Lennon. And these two guys were jamming together and they stopped and I said 'Any chance that you might grace us with your presence on stage?' 'I'm afraid our management wouldn't allow it, otherwise we'd love to', one said, so I said 'You enjoy yourself', and they just disappeared, I don't think anyone really knew who they were, because everyone had

long hair, beards and funny hats and looked like everybody else.
**Colin King, festival show director**

Colin King was the flamboyant festival producer and no one was left in doubt that he was in charge of proceedings. It was he who had booked the bands and dealt with their agents and managers on behalf of the Round Table organisers, and there is no denying that he worked tirelessly throughout the weekend. But the way he dressed and his style of making announcements from the stage was ridiculed by the music press:

Colin King wandered around looking like a faded flower child and insisted, along with some other compères, on trying to turn Weeley into a second-rate Woodstock with embarrassing and totally inadequate ramblings over the microphone.
*New Musical Express*, **4 September 1971**

One story I remember was about Colin King, the music organiser. He was a very flamboyant character and he tended, like a lot of people associated with showbiz, to be dramatic. He went into the communications tent in a great panic and said to Norman Thompson, who was responsible for communications and a member of the Round Table … thumped his hand on the table and said, 'I want a helicopter and I want it now' and Norman very calmly looked at him and said, 'any particular colour?'
**Dr Dick Farrow, Clacton GP and Clacton Round Table**

When Rod Stewart arrived he had on a bright pink satin suit and I was wearing a bright green satin suit of the same cut and design. We both looked at each other and said 'Mister Freedom?' and we said, 'Yep'. We'd both been to this boutique in the King's Road

**Rod and The Faces wake up the crowd.** (Getty Images)

the week before and bought our identical suits. Then Marc Bolan turned up and he'd also bought a satin suit, 'cos it was de rigueur amongst the glam rock brigade. In fact, King Crimson, when they turned up, all wore matching white satin suits of a similar design, and they looked very strange, they had a white Rolls Royce and these white satin suits. They were very peculiar.

**Colin King, festival show director**

Excitement grew throughout the Sunday afternoon as the festival moved towards its climax. Although fatigue was starting to set in, anticipation was high amongst the thousands who had spent all weekend on the festival site waiting for the appearances by two of the biggest glam rock acts of the day, Rod Stewart and Marc Bolan.

Bolan was founder and lead singer of a folk group, Tyrannosaurus Rex. They had enjoyed limited success in the late sixties and had a substantial hippy following, but at the end of 1970 the band's name was changed to T.Rex and, like Bob Dylan six years earlier, Marc Bolan 'went electric', switching to a far more commercial style and targeting a younger, more mainstream audience. Although many traditional Tyrannosaurus Rex fans were deeply hurt by what they saw as the band's betrayal, the change was certainly paying off financially, as their single, 'Hot Love', had spent six weeks at number one in the charts.

Rod Stewart had been around the pop scene for many years and was well known for his lively appearances. He'd recently joined up with former members of The Small Faces, effectively replacing Steve Marriot on vocals. The group was now known as The Faces, and was appearing with Rod at Weeley. He was also on the verge of his hugely successful solo career, with his album 'Every Picture Tells A Story' and double A-side singles,' Reason To Believe' and 'Maggie May' released during that summer. In fact the single was to be issued just days after Weeley.

On the Sunday evening, The Faces were due on at 7 p.m. Midway through the afternoon, the bands were running a bit behind schedule and the DJ tried to get things moving along. I remember a couple of bands who wanted to do encores were not allowed and the crowd weren't too happy with that, but he said, 'well, you want to see The Faces don't you?' and the crowd all cried 'yes' … and then he said, 'you want to see T.Rex don't you?' and the crowd all cried 'no' and booed.

**Keith Page, festival fan**

Both of their managements were, quite rightly, trying to say that they were the top of the pops themselves. Both were in the charts, and so it was very difficult to say one was more important than the other. Each of the management teams were vying for top billing, so I tried to explain to them that there was no top billing because it the festival was on during Friday and Saturday night and Sunday too. It was going on and on and on, and whether Rod played first or Marc played first was kind of irrelevant, but the management weren't having it and they were arguing about fees.

So I managed to get hold of both the guys, with a phone in each hand and said, 'Let's be real about this … I'll throw a coin and whoever gets heads or tails will get to be number one on the Weeley stage.' Of course, it was Marc who won and he got to be on after Rod Stewart, but between them it was all friendly banter. It was just the managements being a nuisance, and of course, when they'd been paid up front, they both gave me a cheque back on stage for the Save The Children fund, so they both gave money back to charity.

Rod Stewart was paid £1,500 and so was Marc Bolan.

**Colin King, festival show director**

My band was called Mustard, and originally Clacton Round Table had wanted us to play, but as it became a progressive music festival and we were more a pop band, we declined the offer. We didn't want to make a fool of ourselves in front of such a huge crowd, but we were backstage for the whole festival. We were there as a band, but didn't play,

but we ended up loaning some of our equipment to bands that needed amplifiers. I chatted with them all, Mungo Jerry, T.Rex, Rod Stewart – he was there in a pink satin suit and arrived in a Rolls Royce. It was just a great time.
**Hoss Selfe, Weeley resident**

**Marc Bolan and T.Rex looking anxious before their stage appearance.**
(Getty Images)

At 7 p.m. on the Sunday, The Faces appeared. Rod Stewart was resplendent in a pink satin suit, no shirt and a scarf. He bounded on to the stage and said, 'Quick tune up and we'll be right wiv yer,' and they were brilliant, Rod had the audience in the palm of his hand. He was strutting his stuff and he was drinking from a wine bottle as he performed. And then he announced one song, he said, 'this is about a schoolboy who falls in love with a dirty old prostitute' and he launched into 'Maggie May'.

**Keith Page, festival fan**

The one act that I really wanted to see, and listen to, was Rod Stewart and The Faces. I made time to get up on the side of the stage to film their performance, and it included the first live performance of 'Maggie May'. I was intrigued that he consumed two bottles of Liebfraumilch during his time on stage … I do hope that his taste in wine has improved since that time.

**Dr Dick Farrow, Clacton GP and Clacton Round Table**

I was on the stage when The Faces were on and I seem to remember Rod Stewart said, 'I've got a new number I want to try out', and of course it was 'Maggie May', and I was just 6ft away from where he was singing. It was very noisy there, but when he started singing 'Maggie May', after about twenty or thirty seconds everything started to quieten down and then it was like going to a Pavarotti concert. Everywhere was an absolute hush, and as I watched and listened, I found it was one of the most moving songs I've ever heard. Most of his stuff was very loud and noisy, but this was absolutely brilliant.

**Nigel Davers, Clacton Round Table**

**'Rod the Mod.'** (Getty Images)

No group generated the excitement of The Faces – fifteen minutes before they went on, the crowds were clapping together empty beer cans or anything they could lay their hands on in anticipation of a good set.

The cans did the trick – The Faces were in a good mood and an audience who half an hour previously had looked like they were about to fall asleep, stood up as the group leapt on stage …

'Maggie May' brought the best response of all [in their set], before the closing number, 'Losing You'. The Faces may have thought they'd finished at that point when they'd played for an hour, but the audience weren't going to let them go.

**Ronnie Wood, Ronnie Lane and Rod Stewart.** (Getty Images)

'Feel so Good' was an excellent choice of encore and it was an amazing sight to see an audience of around 100,000 all standing up and chanting back the chorus line.
*New Musical Express*, 4 September 1971

Eventually Rod and The Faces left the stage with an unspoken challenge to T.Rex – follow that!

It was the turn of Marc Bolan to face his fans, and many critics, who were not so keen on him and his new-found 'Glam Rock' sound, but at least he was washed and dressed for the occasion:

My friend, who lived a little further down the hill to me, came rushing up to see me, her old face a-beaming. 'You'll never believe this,' she said. 'T.Rex had a bath in my house.' They came and asked if Marc could have a bath there. She got a pound.
**Ena Wade, Weeley resident**

My claim to fame, I suppose, is that Marc Bolan and Mickey Finn both came and stood right next to me by the wire fence before they went on, drinking a bottle of vodka or something, a bit of Dutch courage … these two guys, now sadly both dead, were just standing there. I can't remember if I spoke to them. I was 19 at the time, but I just can't remember …
**Tony Haggis, festival fan**

Marc Bolan had 'Hot Love' out in the charts, but before he came on some of the fans were booing him. They were old, original fans, acoustic fans if you like; as soon as he 'went electric,' they tended to disown him and wanted to show that they didn't like it. But when he did get on stage he won them over, and it was fantastic in the end. Seeing the expression on his face, I think he was worried about it.
**Hoss Selfe, Weeley resident**

Marc Bolan came on stage and said, 'You've probably seen me on Top of the Pops. I'm a big star,' and that didn't go down too well with some of the audience.

But anyway, the band played a couple of songs. Then, leaving Marc Bolan to himself, he sat on a cushion with an acoustic guitar and played three songs, including 'Deborah'. Then the rest of the band came back and they played their hits, 'Ride A White Swan', 'Get It On', 'Hot Love' and went down quite well. They played an encore of 'Summertime Blues' and then they were off.

They got quite a good ovation, but nowhere near the response that The Faces had.
**Keith Page, festival fan**

The Faces got a huge reception, they were great, but I remember the crowd booing when Marc Bolan came on. 'You should clap for me, I've been on *Top of the Pops*' – that didn't go down well.
**Robert Day, festival fan**

As if following The Faces' incredible show-stopping performance wasn't more than enough for any band to overcome, T.Rex had to contend with various irritating hang-ups, like equipment failure and a barrage of abuse from certain sections of the crowd, whose feelings towards Mister Bolan's band had earlier been aroused by Mister Un-Cool himself, Colin King.

It would appear that to some, T.Rex have committed the unforgivable and cardinal sin, of becoming popular. With his tongue planted firmly in cheek, Marc stated, 'I'm Marc Bolan, you've seen me on Top of The Pops, I'm a big star'. Unfortunately, some took this as gospel and gave him some lip, to which Marc retorted, 'Why don't you F*** Off'. Eventually, his dissenters were silenced by Marc threatening to leave the stage, 'If you don't want to listen then I'll leave.'

Well, T.Rex didn't leave; instead, they performed a somewhat curious set ... Bolan did about everything except smash his guitar and take off into space.

You can't compare either Bolan or T.Rex to other bands; they are a power unto themselves and an essence that needs savouring on more than one hearing and under far better conditions than at Weeley.
*New Musical Express*, 4 September 1971

I remember the Faces with Rod of course, and then there were T.Rex, who was booed. I don't think they were well liked after their name change and the commercialisation of their music. I eventually went to sleep on that Sunday night to the really weird sounds of Van der Graaf Generator, very strange. I still don't get their music.
**Tim Hillyar, festival fan**

**Steve Currie, Mickey Finn and Marc Bolan of T.Rex.**
(Getty Images)

During Sunday evening, an impromptu press confer-ence was given by Vic Speck for the Round Table, surrounded by journalists from national newspapers; he admitted that some of the Hell's Angels on-site on Saturday had received a pay-out. He told reporters that a number of Hell's Angels had confronted him and other organisers and demanded jobs:

> They came into my tent ... One tends to bow to their demands through sheer weight of numbers. They said they were going to take over security and mentioned a payment of £4 a day. I did not employ them, we absorbed them. Their presence was rather over-whelming and frightening. I felt intimidated and did not want to antagonise them to cause trouble for anyone.

Vic Speck also told reporters that when he was approached by the Hell's Angels he'd been 'noncom-mittal and passed the matter on to Mr Bartholomew, who was now in charge of security arrangements'.

Ron Bartholomew told reporters that he'd made a list of sixteen names of Hell's Angels and told them that 'he'd see what he could do':

> They suggested they looked after the security at the fence. If we'd said no they would have done it anyway, we gave them £5 worth of beer as a peace offering, but there was no agreement about wages. I put them on the fences of the arena. No set rates were arranged. I worked out that they had worked for a morning before the trouble blew up and paid them accordingly. They were given £5 worth of gear (in this case beer) as the traditional peace offering.
> **Ron Bartholomew**

Of the sixteen Hell's Angels who were 'on the list' seven of them each received £4 from the organisers.

Vic Speck also spoke about the festival in general:

I envisage a profit of between £10,000 and £30,000, which will go to ten Clacton organisations as well as four national charities. I have spoken to many of the groups and they say it has been a good festival, a brilliant festival. I would do it again; I am that sort of man.
**Vic Speck, Clacton Round Table**

Representatives of the traders and concessionaires on-site also spoke to reporters, claiming that the security arrangements were woefully inadequate: 'There were no security men here able to handle the situation. The Angels should not have been here.'

The press then turned to the police for answers to their questions. They wanted to know why there appeared to be so few officers on the festival

**Weeley in the news.**

site, and why the fighting was allowed to get out of hand on Saturday afternoon. Chief Constable John Nightingale answered their questions. Hell's Angels and others were being held in custody at police stations in Harwich, Clacton, Colchester and Chelmsford. Those charged would appear in court after the Bank Holiday:

Right from the start, we agreed with the organisers that internal security on the site was their responsibility because it was private property. Secondly, it was generally accepted that the presence of police officers in uniform among the sort of young people who attend these festivals, was not the best way of preserving the peace. Hundreds of police were standing by, however, and the organisers were in touch with the command post by telephone and walkie-talkie radio. We received no information on the situation developing. They could have had us at any incident in less than two minutes ... without Saturday's incidents the number of arrests would have been only about 40. 'We have nothing but praise for the conduct of the majority of people there.
**Chief Constable John Nightingale**

The Bank Holiday Monday morning newspapers once again had Weeley stories on their front pages:

**PAY-DAY FOR THE ANGELS**

**SECURITY ROW AT WEELEY OVER 'GUARDIAN' ANGELS**

**HELL'S ANGELS ARE PAID PROTECTION MONEY**

The editorial pages also made interesting reading, going out of their way to praise the behaviour of the music fans:

Until a handful of thugs muscled in, the great Weeley Pop Festival was impressively well-behaved, even somnolent so don't blame the pop fans for the punch-up.

Their style of dress or undress may not suit everybody. Their standard of hygiene may raise some eyebrows.

Some Hell's Angels and some security men were involved in a fearsome battle at the Festival. A battle that brought terror to Popsville.

If a Hells Angel is making trouble, it's a genuine bobby we want to come along and do his stuff. Not some so-called 'security officer'
**Newspaper extracts**

# 9

# TIME TO SPLIT THE SCENE

And then suddenly it was all over. The music came to an end early on Monday morning, and those on the festival site started to leave. According to the police more than half of them had left by 9 a.m, just three hours after the music finished:

On the morning they left I was lying in bed, this was about 6 o'clock in the morning and all I could hear was this strange 'pitter-patter' sound. I said to Bob, 'whatever's that noise?' I got out of bed and looked out of the window … and it was footsteps. There was all these hundreds of hippies walking down to the station – you couldn't put a pin between them. It was like a river running down the hill. I think British Rail brought in extra trains to get them all home.
**Ena Wade, Weeley resident**

By the end of the festival we'd all kind of lost each other, some had gone home because they were dirty or had run out of money, although we didn't take much money with us … anyway, we'd all lost each other for whatever reason, and me and my chum put our stuff together in our rucksacks and wandered over to the railway station.

Now, we lived in Walton-on-the-Naze, which was in the opposite direction to where everyone else was going, so the two of us walked down and went under the arches on to Weeley station, I suppose this was around 10.30 a.m., and the two of us just stood there, and we were alone on that platform towards Walton, but on the other platform, well it was just unbelievable … there were just thousands of people coming down the fields, all wanting to go on to London-bound trains. Well, of course, they couldn't cope. I think by then they'd seen what was going to happen and had laid on a few extra trains, but it was extraordinary to be sitting there, with a bad head from too much music … and cider, looking over at thousands of people – in a similar state to us I guess, but there were just the two of us on our platform, and everyone else was on the other side.
**Tony O'Neil, festival fan**

Then on Monday morning we were all sort of herded along to the station, and the trains pulled into the platform and there were hundreds of people there waiting for them. This old-style train pulled in, and where I was standing there was a window but no door. I was lighter then than I am now; I just climbed in through the window.
**Trevor Davis, festival fan**

In the information tent, at the end of the festival, there were quite a number of wallets and purses that had been handed in, and they all contained money. Now, what event could you ever go to where a wallet or purse with money would ever be handed in? … I think it showed that the type of youngsters

**The rubbish piles up.**
(Getty Images)

that were there were there not to make trouble but to enjoy their music.
**Graham Syrett, Clacton Round Table**

As 150,000 music fans left their weekend home, the big clean up started, and it was certainly a huge task; paper, cans, fire ravaged vehicles, abandoned tents and clothing, and piles of discarded, rotting food that had been left by the food concessionaires – and worse – had to be cleared away.

Roger Weeley, on whose land the festival had taken place, was complimentary about the festival when speaking to the local press and confident that the clean-up would be handled efficiently:

It was a damn good show and I am quite confident that the Round Table will handle the clearing up as efficiently as they handled the festival.
*East Essex Gazette*, 3 September 1971

When you think of the amount of people who were there, I don't think the mess was that bad. there was a certain amount of damage, but when you think of the amount of people that sat on that field it is to be expected. Cans, beer cans and soft drink cans and paper – paper was the worst thing 'cos it blows about, but it didn't take all that long to clear it up. There was a team of people organised to clear up at the end.

Most of the cars left behind had been burnt or so badly damaged, they were just bulldozed into a heap and taken away for scrap. There was a double-decker bus left behind and we towed it away, and then I actually bought that from the owners and used it for about twelve months for fun and then I sold it on to someone who'd actually been to the pop festival. I towed the bus from the site and stored it and it took me some time to find out who the owner was, it turned out to be Warner Brothers. When I made contact with them, they told me that they had three buses and they were all parked safely in a garage at Richmond, but when they checked they came back to me and said they had one missing, I said, 'Well yes, I've got it.' I told the man that the bus had been left at the pop festival; he didn't seem to understand that. He knew it had been hired, but he didn't know where it had gone, so I explained that it had spent the weekend at the music festival. I then told him that he was going to be charged for towing it off the field and then for storage, he asked me if I'd accept the bus as payment instead, I agreed and he sent me all the documents. I then repaired the engine problems that it had and then drove it round, we used to go to motor racing and various other events, it was quite fun until we got rid of it ... you get rid of cars and you get rid of buses.

Then after the clear up and when we later started ploughing in the field we kept finding coins and penknives for a long time
**David Weeley, Weeley resident, son of Roger Weeley, landowner**

**The mass exodus on Monday morning.** (*Clacton and Frinton Gazette*)

There was a tremendous amount of rubbish left. It was a scene of devastation, really. But it was really surprising just how quickly it was cleared up.

**Mike Sams, newspaper reporter**

They took away lorry loads of bottles and cans and stuff left behind. There were blankets and towels and tents and brollies. They were in such a hurry to go. They left lorry loads of rubbish, absolutely lorry loads.

**Ena Wade, Weeley resident**

**Tired and exhausted.**
(Garry Bodenham)

Weeley station has never been this busy, before nor since. (Alamy)

The amount of rubbish left behind was horrendous, I don't think it was very well organised on that front, simply because they hadn't realised how many people were going to turn up ... and how much rubbish they'd leave behind.
**Hoss Selfe, Weeley resident**

Cleaning up afterwards was a huge task ... at the end of the event, when a few of us were tidying up the site, which was a major problem, he [Bill Leiper, neighbouring farmer] came along with his tractor and helped when we were trying to dig up the water pipes by hand. The ground was completely solid; he dug up the line and pipes for us ...

**The clean-up starts here.**
(Mike Sams)

Rubbish, yes, tons of it, and there'd been some people living on-site for a while and they didn't all use the toilet facilities, some of the woodland and ditches were pretty gruesome.

The fields were burnt, in those days farmers often burnt the straw and stubble after harvest, and that certainly helped, so we just had to go round and pick up the metallic objects, tins etc. We did this for a couple of weekends and then it became too much with our limited personnel, we couldn't do it all so some outside contractors were brought in, so the site was cleaned up by them.
**Graham Syrett, Clacton Round Table**

With the festival at an end, the medical staff were able to stand down after treating a huge assortment of ailments, and the Weeley field hospital was dismantled:

The only issue we feared towards the end was being able to provide a particular drug, Physeptone, a heroin substitute. All the local chemists had run out and I called all the pharmacists I knew; they had none. The police were getting worried, but it was Monday morning and the problem moved on.
**Dr Dick Farrow, Clacton GP and Clacton Round Table**

In the official police report that was presented to the Home Office after the event, the chief constable reported on the number of drug associated arrests at the festival:

I had instructed that there was to be no random searching for drugs on the festival area or its approaches. Members of the forces drug squad were patrolling the area with instructions to deal

**The arena empties and the lighting tower survives.**
(Mike Sams)

with any obvious and flagrant offences. In the event 23 arrests were made for possessing drugs.

To the casual observer there was little or no evidence of drug-taking.
**Official Police Report**

The mood throughout Weeley on the Bank Holiday Monday morning, was one of relief, but in most cases, of pleasant surprise that the village and its residents had survived what they'd originally believed would be a wild, violent and uncontrollable rabble invading their quiet corner of England.

**Essex Police statements – 240 of them.** (Essex Police Museum)

Not only had the Chief Constable stressed how well-behaved and peaceful the vast majority of those attending the festival had been, with the press emphasising the point, but the villagers were also liberal with the praise for the crowds of youngsters who'd descended on their village. Many of those who had been critical of the plans were complimentary about those that attended – even parish councillor Major General F.J. Piggot. He told local reporters of his unexpected pleasure: 'I was agreeably surprised; apart from one person who spoke to me on the telephone I have heard no complaints.'

Other local residents joined in the praise for the festival-goers:

In all fairness I would say they have behaved very well indeed. They have been very polite ... they always said, 'please 'and 'thank you'; I don't think they could have been more courteous. It wasn't too bad at all, even the church was able to stay open. They went into the church but no damage was done. There wasn't a lot of noise either; most of the noise drifted over to Thorpe-le-Soken.
Renee Marshall, Weeley resident

There was even praise for the thousands of fans who were ferried into London's Liverpool Street station by train, with the station's manager telling reporters that, 'they are the best set of travellers we have ever had'.

The police operation was also praised by many, despite surprise being expressed at the Chief Constable's announcement that they were unaware of the clash between the Hell's Angels and others until after the event. However, there were no complaints against any of the police officers that attended, and a number of letters of appreciation were received from residents and festival-goers alike.

# 10

# A FEW BAD VIBES

Despite the overall success of the event, there were some in the village who had not been happy from the start, and several letters of complaint were sent to the county council. A few of the complaints targeted the organisers, but the majority were attacking the county council for allowing such a huge gathering to take place:

Having lost hours of sleep, having had my property turned into an open loo, the smell is appalling, I am wondering how the members of your council who were in favour of it would react to such an experience.

After the deplorable 'festival' of 1970 [Isle of Wight] with its trail of filth, depravity, drugs and raucous noise, I for one would have thought the lesson learned.

The state of the roads was a disgrace to the countryside and took several days to clear, and even so, I had to 'phone the council to clear the tins etc. thrown inside my hedge.

I am writing to protest in the strongest terms ...

My daughter, myself and our dog have been made quite ill having to endure this continuous noise and having three consecutive nights without sleep.

It is with utter disgust and heartbreak for a beautiful countryside shamefully destroyed as the result of the awful pop festival ...
**Complaint letters, Essex Police Museum**

As the vast majority of the festival fans left the site on Bank Holiday Monday, around 200 remained to help with the clean-up. Some of these were festival-goers who were unable to leave the area as they were scheduled to appear before magistrates, and so decided to use the time constructively.

In all, 112 arrests had been made over the weekend; a number of those were reported as being Hell's Angels who had been detained on Saturday and held in cells in various Essex police stations. They were escorted to Colchester Magistrates Court, held in the Town Hall, where a specially convened sitting of Clacton Magistrates was to take place.

The court sat for a total of eight hours, until 10.40 p.m. on Bank Holiday Monday, in order to hear the majority of cases against the Hell's Angels. Largely, the Angels were charged with threatening behaviour likely to cause a breach of the peace, which was denied by all forty-one of them.

The case against two teenage girls was dismissed after the police offered no evidence, the remainder of the defendants were men aged between 18 and 27, and one 14-year-old boy also appeared.

With police officers lining the walls of the court, the Hell's Angels were hand-cuffed in groups of three and packed into the dock. Many of them were bare-chested and heavily tattooed.

The case against the defendants was outlined by the prosecutor, who told the court that after the Hell's Angels had arrived at the festival there began, 'a story of robbery, violence, blackmail and general misbehaviour'. The trouble began, he stated, when some of the defendants took over a Land Rover, which was supposed to be used for fighting fires: 'they were driving around and making a frightful nuisance of themselves and frightening everybody on the site.' Fights between Hell's Angels and the security men followed, in which a number of Hell's Angels received serious injuries. The prosecutor told the court that these assaults were being investigated. Many motorcycles were badly damaged and the Hell's Angels went to the police tent to repair their vehicles. The assistant police constable, who was in charge of the police operations, told them to leave the site, and they were even offered transport by the police. However, the Hell's Angels refused to leave, saying they would find those responsible and settle the matter themselves. Hearing that they intended to take revenge, the police then arrested them. It was indicated that the defendants were given time to think things over in the police tent, but when they refused to leave their arrest was ordered by the assistant chief constable.

The prosecutor went on to describe how the Hell's Angels appeared to have a 'very nasty collection of offensive weapons', including two clubs, a motorcycle chain, a knife, two bottles, two studded arm bands, a heavy buckled belt, a wheel brace and an iron pipe. The court was told that some of the defendants were seen driving fast in convoy in two Jeep type vehicles along an unmade farm road near the festival arena. It was claimed that the defendants were on a firefighting patrol and the Jeep had been given to them to use by the festivals organisers. It was suggested that 'they may not have realised that the weapons were in the back of the vehicles.'

Most of the Hell's Angels were defended in court by one of their number, Dave Hawkes, who had previously been a serving police cadet. He appeared with three stitched red gashes on his face and manacled hands. During the court proceedings, Mr Hawkes clashed with the assistant chief constable. He began by asking, 'Do you know we have never been arrested? We have not been charged, cautioned, or anything. We volunteered to go to the police station to give statements and we have been in custody ever since. Can you positively say that I was arrested?'

Mr Duke replied, 'Yes', Mr Hawkes shouted 'Liar'.

The police chief told the court that he had warned the Angels that if they did not leave the festival site, they would be arrested. He said he repeated the warning later and told them that if they did not volunteer to leave they would be forcibly ejected. To this Hawkes shouted 'You are a bloody liar, you are under oath too'.

Other Angels shouted, 'Framed, Framed, Framed.' Hawkes continued:

Ten of us were put in a cell with one wooden bed, no mattresses and no food until the next morning … These boys did not go looking for trouble. We came up to the festival on our bikes and asked for security jobs, we were asked to keep an eye on the barriers around the arena and to put out fires. It was something to do besides listening to the music. We didn't do anybody violence. They came at us [members of the security team brought in by the concessionaires] with shovels and bars of iron. They fired shotguns at our petrol tanks; two of us got fractured skulls. We have spent years and every spare penny building up these bikes, they are our one and only life, it hurts to see them damaged.

Other Hell's Angels also spoke during the proceedings. One told the court, All we want in the world is our bikes and our girls. We can take being beaten up, and so can the girls, but we won't have our bikes smashed up by anyone.'

The Magistrate, Mr R.A. Barton, acknowledged that the Angels had suffered some provocation, but they had 'taken it upon themselves to remedy their grievance'. In a prepared statement from the bench he said:

> After visits to the site, my colleagues and I feel an excellent spirit prevailed at this festival and the vast majority of young visitors conducted themselves in an exemplary manner. Regrettably, a relatively small contingent bent on destruction, gained admission and this element was responsible for the trouble which arose.

He added, 'We wish to express our sincere appreciation of the admirable manner in which the police carried out their difficult duties'.

The Magistrate then found all thirty-nine remaining Angels guilty as charged. Three were jailed and ten were remanded for reports. Twenty-six others were given fines ranging from £25 to £35, totalling £780.

More Hell's Angels appeared before the magistrates as the court sat again on the following day, where two more prison sentences and more heavy fines were imposed.

The court also dealt with a number of drug offences. One defendant was fined £10 with £5 costs for possessing cannabis. When asked how he was going to pay he told the bench, 'Not a chance.' he was jailed, instead, for fourteen days. In all nearly £1,000 was collected in fines for drug offences at the festival.

# 11

# WHERE DID ALL THE BREAD GO?

Over the next few days the financial calculations were undertaken, and here was the next problem. The headline in the local newspaper broke the story:

POLICE CALLED IN AFTER FESTIVAL CASH SHOCK
Clacton Round Table, organisers of the Weeley Music Festival last weekend, dropped a bombshell yesterday with the shock announcement that they have 'many thousands of pounds less in the kitty than expected' from their mammoth charity event.

A statement issued by the Table added: 'We have now placed the matter in the hands of the police.'

The statement was made on behalf of the Round Table by Mr Peter Gibbs, who was 'number two' to Mr Vic Speck, main organiser of the festival.

'We will not be able to produce final figures for some time yet, as we have not received many bills and there is also money to come in from various sources' said Mr Gibbs, 'But it is already obvious that we are not going to make anywhere near the profit we originally hoped for.'

The statement added that trouble for the organisers came, when numbers arriving at the site escalated almost beyond control, and with over 3,000 people an hour pouring into Weeley, security was hopelessly inadequate and the hoped-for supervision at the entrance was unable to be maintained.

*East Essex Gazette*, 3 September 1971

Although the festival had been seen as a great success by most of those attending, the organisation had been marred throughout by inadequate control of security. It had become obvious that the loss of revenue was again due to lack of security on the entrances to the festival.

Many thousands of tickets had been legitimately sold prior to the Festival and accounted for by the Festival box office, run by Peter Gibbs. More were sold on the gate by members of the Round Table and trustworthy helpers, but some others involved with security and running the gate had not proved to be as honest. There were cases of tickets being copied, others being collected in and resold with the money pocketed, or money taken without tickets being issued. Because of the huge number of people entering the festival site, it became impossible for the Round Table to keep a check on the situation:

I think we took £106,000 and we should have taken £225,000, even though we declared it a 'free festival' after a while ... I can't remember when. I think there were a lot of forged tickets and, although we were all businessmen, we were all green in the 'crooked side of things' such as counterfeiting ... we had no experience of this whatsoever. We all ran businesses in Clacton and all our business was via word of mouth and handshakes, we weren't use to dealing with criminals. The tickets weren't like they are today, it

was just a base ticket and it was copied and I heard these tickets were being sold for 50p each.
**Nigel Davers, Clacton Round Table**

No, it didn't make money. The whole idea of the event was to make money for charity, there was one cheque given out on stage to Julie Felix, a thousand pounds for one of the charities, but after the event when the monies were added up we realised that we might be going to go into a heavy loss situation and all of us, as Tablers would have been individually liable. Fortunately the Round Table movement as a whole backed us totally to the hilt, promising money if we got into that situation. In the end I think we renegotiated some of the bills so we virtually broke even. So we didn't make any money, which was the idea when we went into it.

So, as far as fundraising was concerned it was a part failure, but as far as an event for the locality was concerned, it was a success.

Security was quite a problem, the ticket sales were not under control of the Round Table, and we were overwhelmed.

I had several different tasks and during certain times when I was going around the site, I could see these 'local people' taking the money, helpers, and I thought this should not be, it wasn't a good move.

I think a lot of people did very well out of the festival, sadly not the Round Table or the charities. We should have got more involved in that side of proceedings, but we were in it before we realised, and with that influx of extra people we were simply overwhelmed.
**Graham Syrett, Clacton Round Table**

A lot of tickets were sold and Round Table, who had been naive, lost control, which was very sad, because it would have been wonderful to give a lot of that money to good causes.
**Dr Dick Farrow, Clacton GP and Clacton Round Table**

I often wonder where a lot of it went, because there wasn't quite as much money went to charity as money was taken. I know that there were a lot of people on-site selling fake tickets and taking

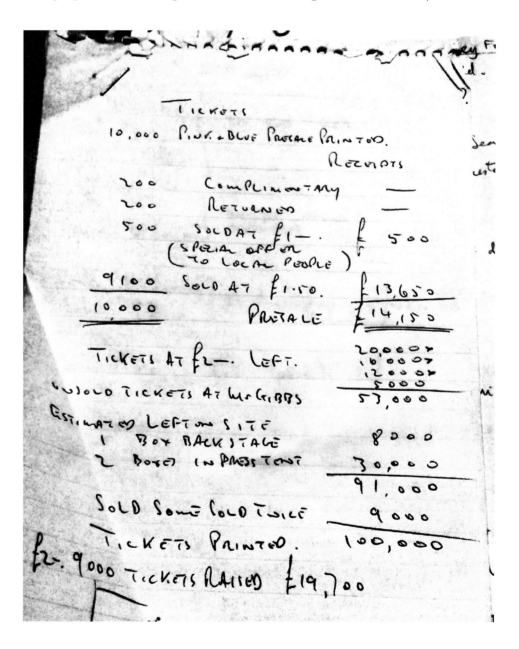

**The 'accounts'.** (Essex Police Museum)

**'This letter clears my conscience ...'** (Essex Police Museum)

money for fake tickets, but I do know that a lot of tickets were sold.

My suspicions are that 'local gangsters' got hold of the money somehow or another, I have no more

than suspicions, but I can say that the guys in the Round Table were absolutely impeccable and anything that went was nothing to do with them. They worked so hard over the weekend – the whole week really – and were real gentlemen, but somehow or another there was something astray. When I went to get my money – after all I was paid for this, that was the idea – I was told that there wasn't any money left, and I didn't really understand ... I did get paid eventually, but it was out of someone's pocket.

I know that there was at least 80,000 tickets sold upfront at £1.50 and I know that I spent £15,000 on the groups, and I don't believe the rest of it was spent on the festival, having made festivals happen and knowing what it costs.

Of course that amount wouldn't go anywhere these days.

**Colin King, festival show director**

A number of notes and letters, some of them anonymous, were sent to the police following the festival, making accusations against certain characters and confirming some of the methods used to trick the Round Table out of the ticket revenue:

CONFIDENTIAL

If you question certain security guards who were employed at Weeley Festival you should obtain some information concerning missing cash.

One or two of these people concerned are quite free with there (sic) talk about what was made selling tickets. In one case it was several hundred pounds.If you contact a person named ....

**Letter to police, Essex police Museum**

Another letter sent to the police gave details of the ticket scam that the sender claimed to have witnessed:

...details of a fiddle which was seen by me at the entrance at the rear of the arena near the toilets the 'Hell's Angels' were employed at this gate to check tickets and deal with security.

The 'fiddle' was to collect the tickets from those who entered and instead of tearing the tickets in two, they were collected wholly.

The tickets were then offered for sale at half-price by other 'Angels' in the approach road to the arena. One ticket could therefore change hands hundreds of times.

I know this information may or may not be of use to you. But to cheat charity is SICK. This letter clears my conscience and I hope will lead eventually with other evidence to some police action.

**Letter to police, Essex Police Museum**

Essex and Southend-on-Sea Constabulary was, in general, praised by the majority of Weeley residents and festival-goers for the way it policed the event. For much of the period of the festival, the officers were positioned away from the more public areas, for fear of enflaming the situation, although the police were full of praise for the majority of those attending the event.

Their delay in attending, and possibly preventing injuries, to those involved in the disturbance between the Hell's Angels and others was criticised, but the police maintained that there had always been an agreement that the Round Table would take control of security of an event that was held on private land. It was stated that 200 police officers were available to control violence on Saturday afternoon, after calls for more officers on-site. Records show that 157 officers were on duty on Saturday evening and 105 PCs were stationed at Weeley on Sunday; a number of CID officers were also in attendance.

The cost to the police force, and ultimately the public, was huge, overtime payments, travelling costs, feeding and welfare costs for the weekend totalled nearly £40,000.

The Chief Constable, who had been on-site for much of the weekend, followed up the festival with an official report covering the policing of the event and observations made during the weekend. The report was presented to the Home Office and included a conclusion. It's interesting to read this part of the report, which would have a bearing on future events of a similar kind, including the huge pop festivals held today:

CONCLUSION
• No festival of this size should be allowed on an arable agricultural site of this sort without the strictest conditions as to the elimination of fire hazards. It is indeed fortunate that in this case no one was burnt to death in the camping area. The combination of tons of loose dry straw, oil and spirit stoves, open fires, plastic tents and a largely uncaring and irresponsible population crammed together was terrifying. Similarly the

**Anonymous note to the police.** (Essex Police Museum)

presence of 60,000 persons or more together at night in an unlit or, at the best, poorly lit, arena with inadequate exits could, if any sort of panic developed, produce an appalling loss of life.

- Of the very large number of people who attended virtually all wished to enjoy themselves in somewhat unusual surroundings and wished to give no trouble to the police or anyone else. It was quite obvious that they were prepared to help each other in any way possible.

- The Hell's Angels also wished to enjoy themselves in their own way. Their main source of enjoyment seemed to be exhibiting themselves as tough guys to the public at large. Unfortunately they also enjoy, and were allowed to have, free beer and this seems to have caused them to assault and threaten others, probably including the organisers. When confronted, even in comparatively large numbers by a few resolute police officers they were amenable. They would cause very little trouble if they did not believe they had some backing from the organisers.

- The so called security staff, remains a bit of a mystery. Originally it was agreed that there would be a security staff in the accepted sense, i.e. persons employed to preserve order and prevent access to various enclosed parts of the site. In fact no such staff were provided and indeed towards the end of the festival the organiser admitted that he only had 'marshals' i.e. persons employed to collect money and check tickets at the various entrances. It had been implied that a 'national security company' would have a security function: in the event this firm played a small part in assuring the safe custody of cash on the site and then only on behalf of the catering concessionaires.

- If such festivals are to be held this trouble of law and order must be faced. It is said that a police presence on the site is unacceptable to the persons attending. I accepted this in the first instance. I am now inclined to doubt it. I do not think a police presence necessary or desirable in the arena, camping or car parking areas; but such a presence ought to be provided in the administration areas backstage and in any area where concessionaires are collected. I think this would be good: I was asked to provide police for the medical tent but declined because I thought this might deter persons in need of treatment from using the facilities provided. I was probably wrong.

- As to the general question of licensing, I am sure that the line taken by the Essex County Council was wrong. The Special Purposes Committee accepted in good faith the applicant's statement of intention to restrict the numbers allowed to attend. When it became apparent that the organisers had neither the ability nor the intention to do this, the officers of the council let matters slide hoping that the organisers would abandon the festival. It now seems that the organisers were so far committed financially that it was impossible for them to withdraw.

- A system of licensing would work if it was limited to granting or refusing an application for the licence and to the imposition of certain regulatory conditions as to fire precautions, security, public health and the like. However, the licence should be granted and such conditions should be imposed in sufficient time, to give the organisers a chance to withdraw. To issue a licence 5 days before an event which has cost many thousands of pounds to stage and to attach to it conditions which the issuing authority knows to be unenforceable, seems to be unwise to say the least. In any event, the present sanctions for breaches of conditions are inadequate. No one seems to be willing to say how much money is involved. The cost of tickets for this festival was £1.50 before the event and

£2.00 at the site. If, as seems to be generally agreed, over 100,000 people attended and 70 per cent (a figure mentioned by one of the organisers) paid, a lot of money was collected. How much was actually passed on to the organisers by the collectors is open to doubt and the organisers themselves do not seem to be very clear about this, but it still must have been a considerable sum. Some of this money may well have been paid out for protection and in other ways but I am sure that if there are any sanctions to enforce a system of licensing they should be very high – in thousands of pounds. A festival such as this is a 'big money' operation.

• A condition of any licence granted to a festival purporting to be in aid of charity should require the presentation of an audited statement of accounts within a reasonable time.

**Weeley Pop Festival Report, Essex Police Museum**

leave taken in conjunction with it was cancelled throughout the Force for the three days 28, 29 and 30 August. The cost of overtime payments throughout the Force for these three days and for the day preceding is about £46,000. Precisely how much of this is directly attributable to the festival is impossible to calculate but that proportion is estimated at approximately 80% i.e. £36,800. Other costs were incurred for catering, transport, travelling, subsistence, equipment, accommodation, civilian staff overtime and other small items. Details are as follows:-

| | £ |
|---|---|
| Police overtime | 36,800 |
| Catering | 730 |
| Transport & Travelling | 482 |
| Subsistence | 611 |
| Equipment | 385 |
| Accommodation | 366 |
| Civilian Staff Overtime | 303 |
| Miscellaneous | 58 |
| TOTAL | £39,735 |

None of these costs is recoverable.

**The cost of policing Weeley.** (Essex Police Museum)

# 12

# GETTING HEAVY

In the following days there was much discussion both nationally and locally about Weeley Festival - and large public gatherings in general. A number of letters critical of the organisers, and the county council, for allowing the event, were sent from individuals and businesses. A petition signed by 183 local residents was also presented to Essex County Council:

We the undersigned residents of Weeley wish it to be known that due to the vast influx of young people into this village, it has caused so much concern that it is strongly recommended that no Pop Festival of any kind should be held in this locality in the future.

One member of Essex County Council, Alderman Stanley Wilson from Saffron Walden, called for the organisers to be held responsible for the costs to the public:

I am sick and tired of words of praise in newspapers, on radio and on television thanking pop fans for their good behaviour.

Little is said about the hundreds of police, firemen and ambulance men who had to work all over the weekend instead of being at home with their wives and children. Most of these worked unwillingly and I want to see the organisers asked to foot the bill which will otherwise fall on the ordinary ratepayer.

I have nothing against young people, I've worked with them all my life but the cost of this festival to the whole of Essex was out of proportion to the money raised for charity.

Alderman Wilson's motion was defeated by more than fifty votes.

The events over the preceding weekend at Weeley were raised in Parliament with a number of MPs clamouring to speak on the matter. One Conservative MP from Ormskirk, Harold Soref, was concerned that music festivals were 'the scene of drug orgies and hippie communes that exploded into bloodbaths … Organised armed hooligans and freelance marauders are rampaging over the countryside as protection racketeers and disturbers of the peace.'

A parliamentary bill was ultimately introduced that was planned to wreck events like Weeley in the future. In 1972, MPs were to vote on the 'Night Assemblies Bill' effectively banning any event, but aimed at music festivals, from continuing throughout the night. There were other aspects of the bill that a number of MPs were unhappy with and it was 'talked out' (various clauses of the bill were discussed at such length that the allotted parliamentary time was exceeded). However, a government working party was set up with the objective of drawing up a code of conduct for future events like Weeley. The committee would speak to all interested parties, local authorities, charities and promoters.

The lessons learned in the medical tent by Round Table member Dr Dick Farrow and his team, and the records he kept, would be part of this project, also shaping the way future large events would operate:

I collated all the statistics, which were gathered by the secretaries, and then I was able to write a paper which was accepted by *The Practitioner*, which was a highly respected medical journal at that time, and from that I was also invited to sit on Her Majesty's advisory committee. This committee produced a book on guidance called *The Pop Festivals Report and Code of Practice*, which was published in 1973. This was the basis for what became the code of practice, so I'm assuming that it still functions today.

Interestingly, my paper was requested from people from all over the world; it was quite amazing. I had a lot of requests from behind the Iron Curtain and I also had a request that I remember very well. I was decorating at home and I was at the top of a stepladder when my wife asked could I take a call; it was from Washington DC. I thought she was pulling my leg, but it was the New York drug abuse organisation. They were interested in my paper and asked if I would possibly go over there and give a talk. Sadly it was difficult at that time because of work and family commitments, but the paper has gone around the world.

**Dr Dick Farrow, Clacton GP and Clacton Round Table**

**The way ahead for festivals. Lessons were learned at Weeley.**

# 13

# PEACE, MAN

Although many in Weeley had experienced one too many pop festivals in their lifetime and certainly weren't prepared to suffer another, there were plenty who had enjoyed what they saw as an exciting adventure in a tiny Essex village where 'nothing ever happened':

No one knew what to expect. Parish councillors as well as shopkeepers in the village were of the idea that there'd be an event for no more than 10,000 people held for charity. They were prepared to give it a go, but of course, once it was on, it soon became obvious that this was going to be an event for many thousands of people.

Now afterwards there was a lot of ... not recriminations, but examinations of the event; the organisers themselves had overstretched themselves. Because it was such a massive event and they weren't properly organised, they came out of it owing several thousand pounds; they fell several thousand pounds short.

The parish council said 'Oh we can't have one of those again, it'll be the last time we have one of those,' but it was a one-off event, you just couldn't repeat it. Some people have said, 'Oh, we'll have another concert,' but you just could not do it. Another festival wouldn't have the atmosphere; the enthusiasm wouldn't be there. It would be organised professionally ... with Weeley, here was a little band of 'unprofessionals' who just wanted to do something different.

As far as I was concerned it was the British Woodstock.
**Mike Sams, newspaper reporter**

I think father would have liked to have had another one, he would say 'we had a bit of a problem here and there, but we could have sorted that'.

Before it happened, when it was first known about, a lot of older people in the village weren't impressed at all. I remember one particular lady, she was really upset, she thought it was terrible, really terrible, you know; the end of the world was coming. But she did admit afterwards that although there were some rather uncouth-looking people around, really there hadn't been any problem, apart from the odd pint of milk being nicked off a doorstep.

It certainly put Weeley on the map.
**David Weeley, Weeley resident, son of Roger Weeley, landowner**

I felt sorry for Roger Weeley really, one of the organisers, he was our squire and he done that for charity, for the Clacton Round Table. There was some villains who went off with a lot of the money, but the old chap himself loved it. 'Wonderful show

Bob', he said to my husband. Weeley was a tiny village in those days. It's changed now, but I would like another one.
**Ena Wade, Weeley resident**

Well, when we heard it was coming to Weeley I think we were all dreading it, but even the church was able to stay open. They went into the church but no damage was done – not like today's yobbos! I don't think there was a lot of trouble at all; I think people were expecting a lot more than there really was.
**Renee Marshall, Weeley resident**

It was just a fantastic event and, for the size of audience, the number of people there, I don't think there was a lot of trouble. I remember it as just one happy weekend all-round, unbelievable … I'd long for it to happen again.
**Hoss Selfe, Weeley resident**

In those days we had about 100 free-range chickens running around everywhere on our land, and we had vegetables in the garden, and that was our living. We were worried that they'd take all our eggs, but they didn't. We lived in fear of the unknown, and it never happened – it was all very peaceful. If we'd have known just how peaceful it would be and just how much enjoyment people got out it then we could have enjoyed it more; it was just fear of what was going to happen.
**Pearl Byford, Weeley resident**

I think it was one of the most beautiful weekends of my life. I got to meet some amazing people from both sides of the spectrum: from the establishment … the guys who came from the free food kitchen at Glastonbury who were real down-hard hippies and the local Round Table who were very establishment.

I felt that I was a bridge between two worlds, and I think that bridge was successfully crossed. Both sides learnt a great deal from each other, so it was one of the seminal moments of my life. I shall never forget it.
**Colin King, festival show director**

Am I glad I was involved? Yes, it was an experience, but I would never want to be involved in running another one. I lost half a stone over three days with the worry and just running around … but I wouldn't mind going along as a guest.
**Graham Syrett, Clacton Round Table**

Weeley Festival changed my life; it was one of the most fantastic experiences of my life. Before the festival I was probably a bit of a square and it gave me a whole new outlook on the music … hippies, that I used to look down on … It changed my life completely; a whole new scope of life. I never realised at that time there were so many happy people around: positive thinking, easy and laid-back. I've travelled the world and seen lots of things, studied and worked with lots of cultures … but I've never had an experience like Weeley. It really changed my outlook in life and it was one of the happiest times I had. It wasn't just two nights; I was on-site for the most part of three weeks. I just couldn't believe how you could get 150,000 people crushed together without fighting and everybody smiling and laughing. We did our best.
**Nigel Davers, Clacton Round Table**

The Round Table is a young male organisation which was set up for its members to have a good time, but at the same time to serve the community and raise funds, and this festival was a very good idea … I think. Looking back that we were a bit naive because we really had no idea how it would turn out, I mean, it just mushroomed out of control in many respects, but I think the original idea by Vic Speck was excellent.

Nevertheless, I will always say that however many people there were there, and people have different views ... 99 per cent of them had a tremendous weekend and one that they will always remember. I will always certainly remember it, it was a great time.
**Dr Dick Farrow, Clacton GP and Clacton Round Table**

As the daily conversation between residents in the village turned to more mundane things and the festival memories started to fade, the various official bodies within the county were still counting the cost of such a huge event. The police bill of nearly £40,000 was by far the largest cost to the county, but the cost for turnout fees and feeding fire crews amounted to £600. Reports by county officials who had visited the site before and during the festival showed a number of breaches of the licensing conditions had occurred:

POP ORGANISERS COULD FACE PROSECUTION
Chairman of Essex County Council's Special Purposes committee, Mr David Llewelyn Jones said it will be up to committee members to decide if there were any serious breaches of the conditions and whether any action should be taken against the licence holder or the Round Table for aiding and abetting.

He added, 'I have no regrets at all that we granted the licence'.

The Bank Holiday festival which attracted 130,000 people was organised for charity by the Round Table, but the licence was granted to Roger Weeley, the owner of part of the site.

'I am just going to wait and see what the county council do. I think it is very unfortunate if they see fit to prosecute ... I think generally speaking the whole thing was excellent. It was very unfortunate that organisation broke down just before the end under sheer weight of numbers'
*East Essex Gazette*, 17 September 1971

A court case followed, and on 1 November 1971 at Clacton Magistrates Court Mr Weeley was convicted on three charges of 'keeping Hall Farm for public musical entertainment without a licence' and two breaches of the licence conditions; exceeding the 10,000 attendance limit and failing to remove straw cuttings from the site.

He was given a conditional discharge for one year on each count and ordered to pay £25 towards the cost of the prosecution. The main organisers for the Round Table, Vic Speck and Peter Gibbs, received similar sanctions.

# AND NOW ...

early fifty years after the pop festival, Weeley is still a small village, although the population in the most recent census of 2011 was 1,768 – double that of 1971. At the time of the festival, the village had a short bypass crossing the railway line next to Weeley railway station and continued through Weeley Heath towards the coast. The railway station is still busy with daily commuters, though it's never seen as many passengers as it did over that busy weekend in 1971, but now the entire village is bypassed again by a faster, more modern road to Clacton.

In the village, there is little evidence now that the festival ever took place, with one exception; a small development of houses has been built in a private road, Festival Close, although this is some distance from the festival site.

The exact area where the Weeley festival took place remains as farmland, with St Andrew's Church in the centre of the site. The old remains of Hall Farm have been demolished. At the time of the festival it was a collection of semi-derelict barns. Many of the hedgerows have been grubbed out, making the fields much larger, but where some trees and bushes have gone, nature has taken back control in other areas with thick copses growing up, especially around the church.

The surviving members of Clacton Round Table are now in their 70s, even the youngest of those attending the festival are probably in their 60s. Most of the

organisers speak with pride of the part they played in this amazing adventure all those years ago. They still become animated and passionate when talking about an event that they see as groundbreaking and audacious. Sadly the initiator of the festival, Vic Speck, died some years ago, but the legacy lives on.

Many of those who lived in Weeley at the time still speak with affection of that bank holiday weekend when an event in their tiny hamlet became headline news around the country. Many minds and opinions were changed through events that took place during the festival. A lot of those who feared the unknown and believed their homes would be overrun by wild, uncontrolled and unwashed youngsters were genuinely surprised at the considerate behaviour of the majority when the crowds arrived.

In most cases, those police officers attending seemed to come through the ordeal with their integrity intact. Several of those who were on duty, now long retired, admitted that their preconceived ideas of the youngsters and their behaviour were misguided, and equally, many of those attending the festival spoke highly of the police and the way they carried out their duties.

The Hell's Angels didn't fare so well from the event. With hindsight it seems that a number of scores were settled in those fields over that weekend. For too long the Hell's Angels had ridden behind their reputation as hard men who answered to no one. They had 'thrown their weight around' with many of the concessionaires and tradespeople at previous events, and the patience of these people had been tried once too often. The fact that the caterers were able to call up a gang of their own 'security men' within a couple of hours suggests that trouble was expected and plans were afoot to sort out the Angels once and for all. The police had also been taunted by the Angels on other occasions and were keen to show the public that no group should be seen as being above the law. The beatings and subsequent legal proceedings against the Hell's Angels tamed them, and never again did they cause trouble on such a scale or take on the security at similar events. History has shown that they were singled out for

**Weeley station is little changed in 2016, though the building is set to disappear soon.**

punishment, both by the gang of security men and the authorities; perhaps, though, they were treated a little unfairly. While many members of the Hell's Angels chapters were arrested and appeared in court, the perpetrators of their injuries just disappeared into the crowds, never to be seen again, nor to have their collar felt by the 'Old Bill'.

Interestingly, there appears to be no record of proceedings being taken against those who helped themselves to large amounts of cash that they'd collected on the gate. Whilst 'assisting' the legitimate money-takers and ticket-sellers of the Round Table, money was misappropriated on a large scale and records show that the police received 'tip offs' naming names of some of those suspected of helping themselves. Just by speaking about the subject to those involved in the organisation and the many locals who attended, the same few names are often mentioned, and these names are the same as those reported to the police at the time.

More than once I was told of a certain few who were suddenly driving new cars shortly after the Weeley pop festival. Maybe there wasn't enough evidence to proceed with an investigation, or perhaps, with policing costs at £40,000, the decision was made to draw a line under events that might have occurred at the festival.

Many lessons learned at Weeley are now part of the rigorous organisational structure that must be in place at similar events. Event security has become a business in its own right, with uniformed staff trained to prevent problems and deal with them professionally if necessary. Caterers must consider health and hygiene regimes that had not been thought of at the time of Weeley, and organisers would be run out of town if they attempted to get away with providing the sort of toilet and hygiene facilities the thousands were expected to use at Weeley.

Dr Dick Farrow and his team were on a huge learning curve when it came to providing medical facilities. Dick's meticulous notes, observations and suggestions were incorporated into the guidelines that still dictate today's events.

Festival-goers certainly expect more when attending the festivals of today. Plastic sheets and straw have given way to glamping and near luxury when it comes to accommodation on-site.

Essex County Council and the county authorities are still involved with allowing huge festivals to operate. Chelmsford, just 40 miles west of Weeley, is the site for one of two 'V Festivals' held every year ... and at least one of those Clacton Round Table members is involved, though not as an organiser. Graham Syrett, now a member of Rotary, attends every year with his colleagues when the crowds have gone home and retrieves the abandoned tents and other property, which are then sold on for the benefit of various charities.

The musicians, like the rest of those involved, are also getting older – some showing it more than others. Members of various bands are no longer with us, and very few of those who appeared still enjoy success at the same level as they did in 1971. Although some artists like Al Stewart and bands like Mungo Jerry still perform, the most obvious survivors are Rod Stewart and Status Quo's Francis Rossi.

Weeley was a moment in time, shared by tens of thousands and, in time, will be forgotten, but if you ever pass those fields, just a short distance away from the busy roads of today, you can, with a little imagination, retain a glimpse of something special.

Public footpaths run through the area and walking the path gives an idea of the size of the site and, if you're lucky enough to view the area from the tower of St Andrew's Church, the layout of the arena area, the festival facilities and the camping sites becomes clear even today.

The farm has different owners now, but a few years ago I walked to the exact site of the festival with David Weeley. We strolled through the fields on a beautiful,

warm August morning, just after the harvest and, as in 1971, the straw was still to be cleared from the field. Other than our voices, birdsong and the distant drone of an aircraft, the peace and quiet was noticeable:

There used to be buildings here, a barn and a yard with stacks and straw, old buildings and stuff ...

The stage stood over there, as the wood is a sort of semi-circle and the stage stood in it, like a natural theatre ...

The catering department was here and then, all over that field, there was where all the tents and cars and people were – all there, and there were cars and tents parked on the other side of the church too, everywhere ...

The toilets were a big hole in the ground with a bit of canvas around them – I didn't pay much

**The only acknowledgment of the festival in the village today.**

**Gateway to the festival site in 2016**

**St Andrews Church, Weeley – more peaceful now!**

attention to them. You didn't have to, your senses would have told you where they were!

Many of the hedges have gone now, but more trees have grown up around the church.

That was the field with the stage in, not very big, but there was a hell of a lot of people in there, it doesn't seem possible that 130,000 people were once in that field.

It's a bit silent now isn't it?

I asked if the event should be marked somchow, should there be a plaque somewhere?

No ... definitely not, definitely not ... it's better in people's memories, not stuck on a post.
**David Weeley, Weeley resident, son of Roger Weeley, landowner**

# AFTERWORD: MY WEELEY STORY

I was just 17 years old and I loved my music. I'd started work in London just ten months earlier and I had money to spend; not much, admittedly, but just enough left after buying my monthly railway season ticket to buy a few chart records. I didn't buy too many albums; they were expensive and seemed to include many long, noisy, 'progressive' tracks that were often boring to me.

When I saw the advertisement in *Melody Maker* for the Weeley Festival of Progressive Music, to be held over the August Bank Holiday, I knew that I needed to be there.

I'd heard of some of the bands, The Faces, T.Rex and Lindisfarne, and I figured that I should get to know some of the others, like Principal Edwards Magic Theatre and Van der Graaf Generator.

Together, with six of my chums, all with shoulder length hair, jeans and teenage acne, we sent off for the tickets. Save 50p on each ticket if you book in advance, said the advert. The tickets arrived, and so, eventually, did Friday 27 August 1971.

Weeley was about 50 miles away. We all lived in Essex and had planned to travel in two groups to the festival. None of us had a car, so it would be by train or bus. The majority of the group were still at school, in the sixth year and on school holiday. I was the only one working and had taken a day off.

The first group would travel to Weeley on Friday morning with tents and cooking utensils. Two of the guys had been on camping holidays with their parents and knew about all that stuff. They would also take everything else we might need on what effectively was to be a weekend holiday: tin openers, kettle, mugs etc.

The remaining two, me and my chum Alan, would join them later on the festival site on that Friday afternoon. As we lived in a more rural part of Essex, our journey would be less straightforward and involve several bus changes, so we would leave carrying all the bulky stuff to the others and we'd just bring the food: fresh eggs, cans of baked beans and loaves of bread. Alan's father was the local postmaster and milkman and ran the village store. He'd offered us a deal: we could help him with his milk round before we left in return for the free supply of food. Great idea …

We set off for Weeley after lunch, making four changes of bus, each leg taking about an hour; we eventually arrived at Weeley at about 6 p.m. There were many others on the bus from Colchester travelling to Weeley, most with rucksacks and tents. Very few had trays of fresh eggs and cans of baked beans as we had!

Once we got into Weeley village, we left the bus and followed everybody else. I have vague memories of going through a gate or check point, but I don't remember walking from the village. We walked past the campsite and straight into the arena, where we picked a spot about 100 yards away and to the left of the stage and sat down. And that's where we stayed, apart from one excursion to the toilets – just once, I think, for I would surely have avoided making that visit any more than necessary.

During the evening, record tracks were being played over the loud speaker system, I remember tracks from *Who's Next*, the Who's latest album, and hearing 'Baba O'Riley' at loud volume as the sun was going down. The spectacle of the tiny Weeley church, silhouetted by the flames from the straw burning in a field in the distance on a glorious summer evening with a sky of maroon and fire red, has remained with me ever since and always springs to mind on hearing the first few notes of that track.

Midnight came and we were away with the first act, Hackensack, who sounded just like the next act, who, to be honest, sounded like the next … I do, though, remember Status Quo performing as day broke. By this time I was cold and tired. I hadn't given much thought to bringing a sleeping bag; I don't think I'd ever slept in a field before. A few more bands came along and a few 'hippy' announcements from the stage but we were both hungry, sitting there with the eggs and the unopened cans of beans, and no hope of finding our friends in the huge crowd.

I don't know if it was me or my friend Alan who, at around 10.30 a.m., asked, 'Shall we go home?'

We travelled home on an empty train, leaving behind all the exciting events at Weeley that were yet to come. And the eggs and the baked beans and our friends with the stove, the cooking utensils and the tents – they could have been anywhere on those fields, along with thousands of others. We had no hope of meeting up with them.

I have few regrets in my life, but I do wish I'd persevered with my visit to the Weeley Festival of Progressive Music. I am reminded of that weekend every time I drive through the village of Weeley – which is quite often – and I still find it amazing that those farm fields were filled with thousands of youngsters, just like me, enjoying a great weekend adventure. How is it possible that we are all now in our 60s?

At every opportunity, I'll always say 'I was there.'

**The author, then and now.**

# INDEX